Life on Earth

Poetic Reflections to Empower
Women and Girls

Maria L. Ellis, BBA, MBA

Ellis Publishing House

Washington, DC, USA

Published 2025

DISCLAIMER

Cover Design: Jennifer Stinson

Editing: Cory Hott

DEDICATION

To all the women who came before us, who carved paths
through silence, struggle, and sacrifice.
To the women of today, who rise with strength, wisdom,
and courage in every corner of the world.

And to the girls who will inherit tomorrow—may you
dream without limits, walk with confidence, and know the
unshakable power that resides within you.
This book is for you. May these words remind you that
your voice matters, your presence is vital, and your light
has the power to transform the world.

TABLE OF CONTENTS

INTRODUCTION

By Maria L. Ellis, BBA, MBA

I am a woman who has lived many seasons of life — as a daughter, a mother, a wife, a business leader, and a seeker of truth. Through each stage, I have witnessed how the strength, grace, and resilience of women shape not only families and communities but the very essence of humanity itself.

This poetry collection is born from that realization — a celebration of womanhood in all its forms: tender and fierce, vulnerable and powerful, sensual and sacred. My intention is to empower women and girls to see their worth, to embrace their individuality, and to honor the divine feminine energy that lives within them.

Every poem in this book reflects the voices, struggles, and triumphs of women who dare to love, to lead, and to rise. It is also a tribute to the generations before us — those who opened the doors of opportunity and courage — and to the young women who will continue the journey toward equality, expression, and self-discovery.

May these words remind every reader that femininity is not a weakness but a radiant force of creation and renewal. May they inspire confidence, compassion, and courage — the cornerstones of an empowered life.

With love and purpose,
Maria L. Ellis, BBA, MBA

THE FUTURE BECKONS

In a world where dreams collide,
Where the impossible resides,
There lies a truth, untold, unseen,
Of how impossible goals make life serene.

For in the pursuit of lofty heights,
We shed our fears and took flight,
The boundaries of the past we break,
To forge a future, we will create.

The present, a mere reflection of old,
A tapestry woven from stories told,
But in our hearts, a fire ignites,
Yearning for more, reaching new heights.

Impossible goals, they simplify,
Strip away the clutter, amplify,
They focus our gaze on what could be,
A life that's transformed, wild and free.

For most of our days are spent looking back,
Trapped in memories, on an old track,
But the future beckons, a blank slate,
Waiting for us to embrace our fate.

So let go of the chains that bind,
Release the dreams within your mind,
Embrace the challenge, embrace the strife,
For impossible goals breathe new life.

They accelerate every stride,

Pushing us forward, side by side,
With determination and unwavering will,
We conquer mountains, our dreams fulfill.

And as we soar on wings untamed,
The past no longer holds us, constrained,
We rise above, breaking through the mold,
With impossible goals, our story unfolds.

Dare to dream the impossible dream,
For it simplifies and accelerates the scene,
Your future awaits, a canvas blank,
With impossible goals, your life will rank.

EMPOWERING WOMEN

In a world where strength resides,
Where dreams, like stars, light up the skies,
A call to women, loud and clear,
To rise above, banish all fear.

Embrace your power, fierce and bold,
Unleash the dreams your heart holds,
For you are warriors, brave and true,
With the strength to make dreams come through.

Let not the doubts or judgments weigh,
For you are destined to pave your way,
Embrace your voice, let it be heard,
Speak your truth, let your soul be stirred.

For in the pursuit of your desires,
You'll find fuel that never tires,
Empowerment flows through every vein,
Igniting brilliance, breaking every chain.

Your dreams, they hold significance,
They amplify your existence,
Unlock the doors, unleash your might,
Illuminate the darkest night.

Let passion guide your every stride,
With resilience, you'll reach the other side,
For you possess a fire within,
A force that cannot be contained or dimmed.

Together, we shall rise and soar,

Breaking barriers like never before,
For when women unite as one,
The world trembles, a new era begun.

So dream, dear women, dream so wide,
Let your aspirations be your guide,
Pursue your dreams, empower your soul,
And watch your life beautifully unfold.

For you are the strength, the light, the flame,
Embodied with power, never the same,
Embrace your dreams, let them ignite,
And shine brightly, illuminating your life.

WISE WOMEN CAST ASIDE
THE SHACKLES OF THE PAST

In a world where change seems out of reach,
Where the existing reality seems to beseech,
Wise women rise with strength and grace,
To build a new model, a better place.

For fighting alone won't mend the flaws,
But wisdom, innovation, and a noble cause,
We gather our courage, our spirits alight,
To create a future that shines so bright.

With hearts ablaze, we envision anew,
A world where love and equality ensue,
We break the chains of the old regime,
And build a new model, like a vibrant dream.

We cast aside the shackles of the past,
Creating a legacy that will forever last,
Boldly we step, with purpose in our stride,
With determination, we won't be denied.

We weave compassion into every thread,
Creating a tapestry where no one is misled,
Empathy and understanding guide our way,
As we build a new model, day by day.

In unity we stand, shoulder to shoulder,
Each voice heard, becoming bolder,
We bridge the gaps, with love as our guide,
Creating a world where divisions subside.

For wise women know, deep in their core,
That change comes not from battles of war,
But by building anew, with love and light,
We make the existing model obsolete, out of sight.

So let us rise, wise women strong,
Together we'll prove that we belong,
With resilience, we'll pave the way,
For a future that's brighter, come what may.

For we never change things by fighting alone,
But through unity, compassion, seeds that are sown,
Empowering each other, hand in hand,
Building a new model, a world that will expand.

So let us march forward, with hearts aflame,
With wisdom as our guide, we'll stake our claim,
For wise women know, it's time to embrace,
A new model that brings love and grace.

IN THE HEARTS OF WISE WOMEN

In the hearts of wise women, a vision unfolds,
Of change that is mighty, of stories untold,
They believe in the power of love and compassion,
To break down barriers and create a new fashion.

Wisdom whispers secrets, known only to few,
That change starts with a belief that is true,
They know that to transform the existing mold,
They must first change themselves, from within their soul.

With empathy as their weapon, they listen and learn,
Understanding different perspectives, they discern,
For wise women know that unity is the key,
To shatter the walls of the old decree.

They gather in circles, in sisterhood strong,
Supporting each other, where they all belong,
Through collaboration, their voices unite,
Creating a force that ignites the light.

They challenge the norms, with courage profound,
Questioning the status quo, breaking new ground,
With intellect and wisdom, they pave the way,
For a future that's brighter, come what may.

Wise women believe in education and knowledge,
For they know it's the key to dismantling the bondage,
They seek empower, to uplift and inspire,
To educate generations, to reach higher and higher.

They advocate for justice, for equality and rights,

Fighting for those silenced, for their voice to ignite,
They march in the streets, with banners held high,
Demanding change, with a unified cry.

But wise women also understand the power of peace,
That change can be achieved without violence's release,
They use their words, their kindness and grace,
To bridge the divides, in this tumultuous space.

They cultivate love, in every step they take,
Knowing that unity can undo the existing mistake,
With open hearts and open minds, they succeed,
In building a new model, where all souls are freed.

So let us learn from wise women, their ways,
In their footsteps, we'll walk, through life's maze,
For change can be achieved, when we believe,
That the existing model can be made obsolete, we perceive.

With love as our guide, and wisdom as our light,
Together we'll soar, reaching new heights,
For the power to change lies within our hands,
As wise women, we'll build a future that expands.

WOMEN ADVOCATING
FOR EQUAL RIGHTS

In the quest for change, women stand tall,
Advocating for rights, breaking down the wall,
With voices like thunder, they fiercely proclaim,
The causes they fight for, in passion's flame.

Equality, they demand, in every sphere,
For women's worth to be crystal clear,
They battle against biases, deeply ingrained,
To dismantle the barriers that still remain.

Women advocate for justice to prevail,
In a world where fairness often seems to fail,
They fight against discrimination's grip,
For every woman's right to fully equip.

They champion for women's bodily autonomy,
To make choices freely, without hypocrisy,
Reproductive rights, they fiercely defend,
In the pursuit of freedom, they ascend.

Women strive for safety, for freedom from harm,
In a world where violence can cause alarm,
They raise their voices against abuse and assault,
Demanding respect, for the wounds to halt.

Education, they champion, for all to receive,
To empower minds, to help them believe,
In knowledge's power, to shape their fate,
And break the chains that perpetuate.

Women advocate for the environment's care,
For a sustainable world, they're fully aware,
They fight for Mother Earth, with all their might,
Preserving her beauty, day and night.

They march for peace, for an end to war,
For a future where conflicts exist no more,
With open hearts, they bridge the divide,
Seeking harmony, with love as their guide.

Women advocate for diversity and inclusion,
For acceptance and respect, without confusion,
They celebrate differences, embrace them all,
Creating a world where everyone stands tall.

In their quest for change, women unite,
Supporting each other, shining bright,
With strength and resilience, they pave the way,
For a future where equality holds sway.

So let us stand with women, side by side,
In their fight for justice and equality's tide,
For when women's voices are heard and seen,
A world of change and progress will gleam.

BIG AUDACIOUS LIFE GOALS

In the realm of dreams, where possibilities reside,
Big Hairy Audacious Goals, our hearts confide,
They beckon us to step beyond the known,
To disrupt our lives and make the extraordinary our own.

With courage as our guide, we dare to envision,
A future self and life that defies convention,
These goals, audacious and bold, ignite the fire,
To transcend limits and reach higher and higher.

They challenge us to break free from the norm,
To embrace uncertainty and weather the storm,
For it is in disruption that true growth is found,
Unleashing the potential that lies deep, profound.

With every step taken, we shed the old skin,
Embracing discomfort, as the journey begins,
We shatter the chains of mediocrity's hold,
And carve a path towards a future untold.

Big Hairy Audacious Goals demand our all,
They push us to rise, to stand tall,
They fuel our passion, ignite our drive,
Awakening the spirit within, so alive.

They propel us forward, with unwavering might,
To challenge conventions, and rewrite,
The story of our lives, with purpose and zest,
Creating a future that stands out from the rest.

In their pursuit, we find strength we never knew,

Resilience and determination, shining through,
They teach us that failure is but a stepping stone,
To learn, adapt, and continue to hone.

Big Hairy Audacious Goals disrupt the mundane,
They inspire us to break free from the chain,
Of ordinary existence, of settling for less,
To embrace the extraordinary and truly progress.

WOMEN VISIONARIES DARE

In the realm of dreams, where visionaries dare,
Big Hairy Audacious Goals, with purpose declare,
They ignite a flame, a passion deep within,
Inspiring us to act, to strive and to begin.

These goals, colossal and audacious in their might,
Guide us towards a future, shining bright,
They beckon us to tackle challenges grand,
And extend a helping hand, across every land.

With boundless ambition, they push us to explore,
Innovate, discover, and open new doors,
To seek solutions to problems that persist,
And uplift mankind, with a compassionate twist.

Big Hairy Audacious Goals, they hold the key,
To unlock the potential, in you and me,
They inspire us to unite, to collaborate,
To make the world better, to alleviate.

They call us to bridge divides, to erase the lines,
To foster understanding, where harmony shines,
To embrace diversity, with open hearts,
And build a future, where compassion imparts.

These goals inspire us to heal the Earth,
To protect its beauty, its intrinsic worth,
To nurture nature, in all its splendid form,
Preserving the planet, for generations unborn.

They propel us to fight for justice and rights,

To break the chains of inequality's might,
To empower the marginalized, the oppressed,
And create a world where all are truly blessed.

Big Hairy Audacious Goals, they fuel our drive,
To change the world, to make it thrive,
With unwavering passion, we march ahead,
Embracing the challenges, no matter how widespread.

They remind us that together, we are strong,
That unity can conquer any wrong,
They inspire us to dream, to dare, to act,
Leaving a legacy, impacting every fact.

THE POWER OF INTENTION

In the realm of possibility, where dreams reside,
I stand, defiant, ready to stride,
With intention clear, and passion untold,
To shatter the chains of mediocrity's hold.

No longer confined by the ordinary and plain,
I'll carve a path, where greatness shall reign,
A future abundant, with health, wealth, and bliss,
Where limitations dissolve, and limitations dismiss.

I'll break free from the shackles of doubt,
And embrace a mindset, where possibilities sprout,
With courage as my armor, and resilience my guide,
I'll venture forth, with unwavering stride.

In pursuit of a healthy existence, I'll thrive,
Nurturing my body, so it may revive,
With nourishing choices, and self-care in tow,
I'll embrace wellness and let my inner light glow.

A wealth that transcends mere material gain,
A richness of spirit, devoid of all stain,
I'll seek knowledge and wisdom, with eager delight,
Investing in growth, both day and night.

But wealth not just for me, a shared delight,
For in uplifting others, true abundance takes flight,
I'll build bridges of opportunity and support,
Empowering others, their dreams to escort.

And happiness, a beacon, burning bright,

A reservoir of joy, that ignites pure delight,
I'll cultivate gratitude, in each passing day,
Finding bliss in the simplest of ways.

I'll celebrate uniqueness, in all its forms,
Embracing diversity, weathering storms,
For a future that's inclusive, where hearts intertwine,
A tapestry of unity, where love's light shall shine.
So let us break free, from mediocrity's grasp,
And embark on a journey, where greatness will clasp,
A healthy, wealthy, and happy future we'll mold,
As we shatter the chains, with a spirit bold.

AN EDUCATED WOMAN,
A FORCE OF NATURE

In the realm of wisdom, where knowledge blooms,
Resides a power that transcends all rooms,
A force of nature, fierce and unyielding,
The wise and educated woman, her influence revealing.

With grace and strength, she stands tall and proud,
Her intellect shining, like a vibrant cloud,
She weaves a tapestry of wisdom untold,
Empowering others, as her story unfolds.

Through her words, she sparks enlightening flames,
Igniting minds, erasing societal claims,
She breaks the chains of ignorance's hold,
And nurtures dreams, as they begin to unfold.

Her voice, a beacon of inspiration and hope,
Guiding others up the mountainside slope,
She shares her knowledge, without hesitation,
Creating a world of endless elevation.

She lifts others up, with unwavering support,
A mentor and guide, in a world that can distort,
She sees the potential, in each soul she meets,
And encourages them to rise, to reach their feats.

With her wisdom as a lantern, she paves the way,
For dreams to flourish, in the light of day,
She fosters growth, with love and care,
Creating a community, where dreams can dare.

Her presence, a testament to resilience and grace,
A role model for all, in every time and place,
She empowers others, with her wisdom's embrace,
A beacon of strength, leaving no trace.

For the wise and educated woman, her power is vast,
An advocate for change, in a world that's vast,
She uplifts others, with her knowledge and skill,
Supporting dreams, with a love that's real.

So let us celebrate, the wise and educated soul,
Whose influence and impact make us whole,
For she empowers others, with her wisdom's gleam,
And supports their dreams, like a flowing stream.

BREAKING THE CHAINS OF
IGNORANCE & POVERTY

In a world colored by ignorance's stain,
Where poverty's chains create endless pain,
There shines a beacon, a woman so wise,
An educated spirit, she defies.

With knowledge as her sword, she takes her stand,
Breaking the chains with a determined hand,
She rises above the shadows of despair,
A symbol of hope, with a heart that cares.

In classrooms and libraries, her mind expands,
Seeking wisdom's light, she understands,
That education is the key to break free,
From the shackles of poverty's decree.

With each book she reads and each lesson learned,
Her spirit ignites, her passion burns,
She knows that through knowledge she will rise,
And unravel the secrets that poverty defies.

She refuses to accept the fate assigned,
To be bound by circumstances, confined,
She paves her own path, with resilience strong,
Creating a future where she truly belongs.

Armed with the power of her educated mind,
She challenges the barriers, leaving them behind,
She breaks the cycle, for her children to see,
That education is the key to setting them free.

With courage and grace, she stands as a guide,
For those who still struggle, by poverty's side,
She shares her knowledge, she lends a hand,
Empowering others to take a stand.

Through her actions, she plants the seeds,
Of hope and possibility, fulfilling needs,
She breaks the chains of ignorance and strife,
And opens doors to a brighter life.

So let us celebrate the educated woman,
Who breaks the chains, with a spirit human,
She uplifts others, with her wisdom's might,
And shines a beacon of hope in poverty's night.

For her journey, we find inspiration,
To fight for education, without hesitation,
To break the chains that hold us down,
And create a world where equality is found.

THE POWER OF WOMEN

In unity's embrace, we find our might,
The power of the collective shining bright,
For in our hands, the seeds of change reside,
A future where equity and justice coincide.

Together we stand, women, girls, and more,
Education expansive spirits at our core,
Bound by the belief that all deserve,
A world where every voice can be heard.

Through solidarity's bond, we break the chains,
That silence marginalized, causing pains,
We raise our voices, united and strong,
Advocating for rights that have been too long gone.

In the world of diversity, we weave,
A vision of inclusivity, where all can achieve,
Every color, every creed, every voice,
Coming together, we make a choice.

To dismantle the systems that perpetuate,
Injustice and discrimination, we negate,
For true power lies not in a single hand,
But in the collective, where we all stand.

We uplift each other, through support and care,
Creating spaces where dreams can be shared,
We empower the silence, giving them a voice,
And celebrate their strength, their unique choice.

No longer will we accept the status quo,

We challenge the norms that keep us low,
For in the collective, we find the force,
To reshape the world's flawed discourse.

With determination in our hearts, we strive,
To ensure every person can truly thrive,
A future that's equitable, just, and fair,
Where the power of the collective is everywhere.

So let us join hands, in solidarity's embrace,
Working together, we'll leave a lasting trace,
A world where women, girls, and all can be,
The architects of the future that sets us free.

In unity, we'll create a brighter day,
Where barriers crumble and prejudice fades away,
The true power of the collective, we'll unfurl,
Creating a world where all can truly soar.

WOMEN FOR EDUCATION, LOVE & PEACE

In the realm of education, they ignite the flame,
Collective women rise, determined to proclaim,
That knowledge shall not be confined or denied,
For every girl, a chance to learn, to stride.

They march forward, breaking barriers with might,
For education is a beacon, a guiding light,
They build schools, open doors wide,
Empowering minds, nurturing the inside.

In classrooms filled with love, they sow the seed,
Of compassion and understanding, the world in need,
They teach the lessons of empathy and grace,
Instilling values that transcend time and space.

Through words and actions, they spread the love,
A force that connects, like stars above,
They embrace diversity, celebrate each voice,
Creating a tapestry where all hearts rejoice.

With open arms, they embrace the broken,
Mending wounds, words softly spoken,
They heal the scars of war and strife,
Replacing hate with love, breathing life.

In the quest for peace, they stand as one,
Collective women unite, their mission begun,
They march hand in hand, hearts intertwined,
Demanding justice, a better world to find.

They bridge the divides, build bridges of peace,
Seeking harmony and unity, hatred's release,
Through dialogue and understanding, they strive,
To create a world where love can thrive.

In the actions of the collective, a symphony plays,
Education, love, and peace in harmonious ways,
With courage and resilience, they pave the road,
Advocating for a future that love and peace bestow.

So let us join their noble cause, hand in hand,
Embracing education, love, and peace's demand,
For it is through collective action we can achieve,
A world where every soul can flourish and believe.

WOMEN ACHIEVING
THE IMPOSSIBLE

In the realm of intention, where dreams take flight,
There lies a power, shining ever so bright,
For within our minds, a seed is sown,
The power to achieve what's once unknown.

In the blink of an eye, 90 days unfold,
A challenge embraced, a story yet untold,
With determination, we set our sights high,
To achieve the impossible, reach for the sky.

With every breath, we fuel our desire,
To grow and transform, to reach higher,
For in the science of achievement, we find,
That time is not a barrier to the brilliant mind.

In 10 years of growth, compressed to mere days,
We unlock our potential in remarkable ways,
Through focus and strategy, we pave the way,
Breaking through limits, seizing the day.

The power of intention, a force so strong,
Ignites a fire within, where dreams belong,
With clear vision and unwavering belief,
We conquer obstacles, surpass all grief.

We harness our strengths, confront our fears,
Leaving behind doubts, shedding all tears,
For in the pursuit of impossible goals,
We find resilience, the strength of our souls.

Through dedication, discipline, and drive,
We make the impossible come alive,
With grit and perseverance, we rise above,
Unleashing our potential, boundless like a dove.
In the realm of achievement, time is but a frame,
For the power of intention, it knows no shame,
So let us embrace this science, this art,
And unlock the greatness within our heart.

With 90 days of focus, passion, and zest,
We achieve the impossible, we are truly blessed,
For when intention aligns with unwavering will,
We unlock the magic, and our dreams fulfill.

Dare to dream big, aim for the sky,
Embrace the power of intention, let it fly,
For in the science of achieving the impossible,
We discover our true potential, unstoppable.

EMBRACING IMPOSSIBLE GOALS

In the realm of women, where strength resides,
A journey unfolds, as dreams collide,
When they embrace science, bold and wise,
Impossible goals, they begin to realize.

With hearts afire and minds that soar,
Women discover what lies in store,
In the pursuit of dreams, they find their voice,
Unleashing power, making their choice.

They break the barriers, shatter the glass,
Embracing challenges, they boldly amass,
For in the science of achievement, they see,
The boundless potential that sets them free.

They discover resilience, deep within,
A fire that burns, refusing to dim,
Through setbacks and trials, they rise anew,
With every obstacle, their strength renews.

They find determination, fierce and untamed,
A driving force that cannot be tamed,
With unwavering focus, they forge ahead,
Defying limits, leaving no path unthread.

They discover courage, from deep within,
To face their fears, where growth begins,
Through doubts and uncertainties, they stride,
With confidence and grace, they can't hide.

They find empowerment, a force so strong,

In the sisterhood that propels them along,
Together they rise, hand in hand,
Supporting each other, a united band.

They discover resilience, deep within,
A fire that burns, refusing to dim,
In the science of achieving the impossible,
Women find strength, unshakeable and unstoppable.

So let them embrace this science, this art,
And unlock the greatness within their heart,
For in the pursuit of impossible goals,
Women discover their power, their souls.

With every step, they break new ground,
Innovating, creating, leaving their mark profound,
For when women embrace the science of achievement,
They reshape the world with their relentless commitment.

So let them soar, let their dreams take flight,
Embracing science, shining so bright,
For when women unite, embracing the impossible,
They discover their strength, their purpose, and all that is
possible.

SISTERHOOD EMPOWERMENT

In the realm of sisterhood, a bond so true,
Women find empowerment, a strength anew,
A collective force, unbreakable and strong,
In sisterhood, they find where they belong.

Through shared experiences and stories told,
Women unite, their spirits unfold,
In this sacred circle, they find solace and trust,
A support system that lifts them when they must.

When one falters, others lend a hand,
A network of love, a sisterhood's strand,
They lift each other up, never let one fall,
In the sisterhood's embrace, they stand tall.

In moments of doubt, when darkness descends,
The sisterhood's light, it never bends,
They offer guidance, wisdom, and care,
A haven where they find strength to bear.

In this sisterhood, they find their voice,
Amidst a world that may try to silence their choice,
They speak their truths, unapologetically,
Encouraged and supported unconditionally.

They celebrate each other's victories, big and small,
In the sisterhood's embrace, they stand tall,
No competition or envy, only love and pride,
A sisterhood's bond, forever by their side.

Through trials and tribulations, they navigate,

With sisters by their side, they can relate,
They find encouragement when skies turn gray,
In the sisterhood's arms, they find their way.

So let sisterhood be a guiding light,
A source of empowerment, shining bright,
For in this sacred bond, women find their power,
A support system that will never sour.

In the sisterhood's embrace, they find peace,
A sanctuary where all their worries cease,
Together they rise, united and strong,
In sisterhood, where they truly belong.

So let the sisterhood propel them along,
With love and support, they will forever be strong,
United they stand, hand in hand,
In sisterhood, empowered, they'll forever stand.

CREATE THE CHANGE
THAT WE WANT

In the realm of change, a power untold,
It lies within us, women bold,
For change won't come if we simply wait,
It's in our hands, our fate to shape.

No longer bound by the chains of the past,
We rise as warriors, determined and steadfast,
This is our time, our moment to ignite,
To create change, shining bright.

With hearts ablaze, we dare to dream,
To challenge the norms, to break the seam,
No longer confined by society's mold,
We forge our path, courageous and bold.

We are the change, the force to reckon,
Through resilience and strength, we beckon,
With every step, we pave the way,
For a future where equality holds sway.

In unity, we stand, hand in hand,
Building bridges, across every land,
No boundaries can contain our might,
As we fight for justice, day and night.

We silence the doubts, the voices that say,
That change is impossible, it's not our way,
For we women hold the power within,
To create a world where all can win.

It starts with us, the change we seek,
In every word, every action we speak,
With compassion and love as our guide,
We break the barriers, side by side.
Let our voices rise, like a roaring tide,
As we empower and inspire, far and wide,
For this is our time, our opportunity,
To create the change, we want to see.

So let us stand tall, unyielding and strong,
Together we'll triumph against all wrong,
For we women are the change we seek,
And with our passion, the future we'll reshape.

LIFE TWISTS AND TURNS

Like a river's flow, with twists and turns,
Life presents challenges, sometimes it churns,
But it's in our response, where lies the key,
To navigate the waters, with grace and glee.

Once, a sparrow perched on a withered tree,
Its branches frail, a sight to see,
A storm approached, dark clouds gathered near,
But the sparrow stayed calm, devoid of fear.

The wind blew fiercely, the tree began to sway,
Yet the sparrow remained, not led astray,
It flapped its wings, with courage unfurled,
And soared higher, above the tumultuous world.

In a bustling city, amidst the noise and strife,
A young artist painted, seeking meaning in life,
With every stroke, she expressed her soul,
Creating beauty, despite life's toll.

One day, her masterpiece was torn apart,
By critics, who pierced it with poisonous darts,
But the artist smiled, undeterred by their scorn,
And painted anew, a masterpiece reborn.

A wise old oak, rooted deep in the ground,
Withstood the seasons, its strength profound,
As storms raged and wind howled with might,
The oak stood tall, unyielding to the fight.

Life's trials and tribulations may come our way,

But it's our response that shapes each day,
Like the sparrow, let us rise above,
And find strength in the face of any stormy bluff.

When faced with adversity, like the artist bold,
Let us create beauty, stories yet untold,
And like the mighty oak, let us stand tall,
Enduring life's challenges, through it all.

For life is 10% what happens, they say,
And 90% how we respond, come what may,
So let us choose resilience, with hearts aglow,
And make each moment count, as we grow.

THE POWER TO SOAR

In the realm of parables, a tale unfolds,
Of sparrows and women, courageous and bold,
For in their response lies a lesson profound,
Of strength and resilience, that knows no bound.

Once, a sparrow perched on a fragile tree,
As storm clouds gathered, it faced uncertainty,
The winds howled fiercely, threatening its nest,
But the sparrow remained calm, it passed the test.

With wings unfurled, it soared high above,
Defying the storm, with unwavering love,
For in its response, it found inner peace,
And embraced the chaos, with a heart at ease.

Just like the sparrow, women face life's storms,
With grace and determination, in all its forms,
Through trials and challenges, they steadfastly tread,
Finding strength within, as their spirits are fed.

In a world that often seeks to silence their voice,
Women rise above, making a choice,
To respond with resilience, when faced with strife,
And rewrite the narrative, transforming their life.

Like a phoenix, they emerge from the ashes,
Reclaiming their power, breaking old stashes,
With every setback, they find a new way,
Their response, a beacon, leading the day.

In the tale of the sparrow, we find the key,

To unlock the potential that lies within thee,
For it's not the storm that defines our path,
But how we respond, with love and with wrath.

So let us celebrate the sparrows and women alike,
Their response to life's challenges, a shining light,
May we learn from their stories, and be inspired,
To face our own storms, with hearts untired.

For in our response lies the power to soar,
Above the storms that life may have in store,
Embracing the chaos, with courage and grace,
Women and sparrows, leaving a lasting trace.

In the parables of life, we find the truth,
That our response, no matter our youth,
Can shape our journey, with each passing day,
And lead us towards a brighter, resilient way.

LIFE'S FRAGILITY

In the realm of parables, a tale unfolds,
Of life's fragility, as the story beholds,
For in its brevity lies a truth so clear,
The finality of death, drawing near.

In the Egyptian book of the death, a parable we find,
Of a delicate flower, kissed by the wind,
Its petals so vibrant, its beauty so grand,
Yet destined to wither, held in fate's hand.

Like the flowers, our lives bloom and grow,
In a world filled with joy, and sometimes woe,
We dance in the sunlight, and weather the storm,
But in the end, we all face death's form.

A parable whispers of a bird in flight,
Soaring high in the heavens, its wings shining bright,
Its song fills the air, with melodies sweet,
But its journey is finite, its destiny complete.

So too, our lives are like birds in the sky,
With dreams and aspirations that reach so high,
But as the final note of our song is sung,
Returned to the earth, where our journey begun.

In the book of the death, a parable is told,
Of a river that flows, so tranquil and bold,
Its waters meander, with a gentle embrace,
But even the river must find its own place.

Our lives, like the river, flow with grace,

Navigating through time, leaving a trace,
Yet as the river merges with the vast sea,
We too shall find our eternal destiny.

And in the parables from the book of the death,
We learn that life's fragility is no jest,
For each moment we have is precious and rare,
A reminder to cherish, to love, and to care.

So let us embrace the fleetingness of life,
With gratitude and joy, amidst the strife,
For in the finality of death's embrace,
We find the beauty of living, in every trace.

In the parables of life and death, we see,
That our time on this earth is but a decree,
But in how we live, and in how we love,
We leave a legacy, soaring high above.

So let us cherish the fragility of life's breath,
And honor the finality of death's quest,
For in this dance between life and its end,
We find the essence of what it means to transcend.

LIFE'S PARABLES

In the realm of parables, wisdom does reside,
Lessons woven within each story's tide,
They teach us of life, its beauty and strife,
And the profound mysteries of death's afterlife.

Through parables, we learn of seeds sown,
Of hope and potential in each one shown,
For like the seeds, we too possess within,
The power to grow, to flourish, to begin.

The parables teach us of love's pure might,
A flame that burns bright, illuminating the night,
They show us the value of compassion and care,
And the profound impact of kindness we share.

In the parables, we find tales of forgiveness,
Of letting go, releasing burdens with tenderness,
They remind us that grudges hold us back,
And that forgiveness mends the soul's crack.

Through parables, we understand the fleetingness,
Of life's moments, its joys and its sadness,
They urge us to seize each passing day,
To embrace the present, come what may.

The parables whisper of humility's grace,
Of finding strength in a humble embrace,
They teach us to be mindful of our pride,
And to treat all beings with love, side by side.

In the parables, we glimpse the cycle of life,

The seasons of change, both joy and strife,
They remind us of the impermanence we face,
And the importance of cherishing each embrace.

Through parables, we confront the fear,
Of death's arrival, drawing ever near,
They show us that death is a part of our story,
And that life's purpose is to seek eternal glory.

The parables guide us to seek wisdom's light,
To strive for truth, and to follow what's right,
They teach us to live with integrity and grace,
And to leave a legacy that time cannot erase.
So let us heed the parables' wise voice,
Embrace their teachings and make the choice,
To live a life of purpose, love, and worth,
Embodying the lessons of parables' rebirth.

For in the stories told, we find our way,
Navigating the depths of life's grand ballet,
And when our time on this earth does cease,
We'll find solace in the parables' eternal peace.

FRIENDSHIPS' MEMORIES

In the heart of the bustling New York City,
Amidst the grandeur and the grit,
There lies a place of camaraderie,
The Harvard Club, where friendships are lit.

As I sit here, savoring my morning meal,
I glance around, a bittersweet sight,
For many faces are unfamiliar, surreal,
Reminding me of friends who've taken flight.

Oh, how I miss those great souls,
Whose laughter once filled these halls,
Now departed, beyond earthly roles,
Their absence echoes through these walls.

In this moment, I am reminded,
Of the preciousness of love and time,
To express appreciation, unblinded,
Before their departure to realms sublime.

Let us be grateful for the memories we hold,
For the moments shared, the stories untold,
Cherishing bonds that never fade,
Even as our dear friends have gently wade.

So, raise a toast to those we miss,
To the Harvard Club, where memories persist,
May their spirits soar in celestial bliss,
As we honor their legacy, love, and reminisce.

A CELEBRATION OF ACHIEVEMENTS

In a world where women's voices unite,
Networking becomes a beacon of light.
For in this space, connections are made,
And barriers shattered, like a cascade.

Recognizing each other's life and career,
A celebration of achievements we hold dear.
Empowering one another, lifting us higher,
Together we bloom, fueling our fire.

Through the power of networking's embrace,
We find strength, resilience, and grace.
Sharing wisdom and knowledge with pride,
Women's achievements cannot be denied.

In this sisterhood, we find inspiration,
Supporting dreams and aspirations.
For each milestone reached, we stand tall,
Encouraging others to give it their all.

Let us forge bonds that cannot be broken,
Acknowledge the path that each has spoken.
In women's networking, we find our might,
Uniting for progress, shining our light.

So let us rise, unshaken and bold,
A sisterhood of stories yet untold.
In women's networking, our futures ignite—
Together we ascend, blazing trails of light.

SELF-DOUBT & INADEQUACY

In the depths of doubt, I sometimes reside,
A feeling of inadequacy by my side.
Though I've helped many women and young girls find their
own path to succeed,
In my own self-worth, I struggle to believe.

What is it that I am missing, I ponder,
Why do I feel that I am not stronger?
For my accomplishments, I should surely feel pride,
Yet the shadows of doubt still do subside.

To feel enough, it takes more than success,
A journey within, a quest to address.
Acknowledge your worth, embrace it with grace,
Let go of comparisons, find your own pace.

Remember that you're more than enough,
Your presence alone brings light to the rough.
Release the expectations and judgments that bind,
Embrace your uniqueness, your heart will unwind.

You are a guiding light, a beacon of hope,
Your impact, unseen, helps others to cope.
Trust in your journey, embrace the unknown,
And in your own greatness, you shall be shown.

So let go of doubt, embrace your own worth,
Discover the strength that lies deep in your birth.
For helping others, you're helping yourself,
And in the depths of your soul, you'll find true wealth.

A THANKFUL HEART

In the embrace of a sunny spring day,
In the heart of a city that dances and sways,
I find myself reflecting on life's grand scheme,
As I near the end, like a fading dream.

In the year 2024, the world still aglow,
New York City, my haven, where I watched it all grow.
From a cold winter's day in 1970, I arrived,
To a place that embraced me, where dreams thrived.

As I reach my final days here on Earth's floor,
Gratitude fills my heart, like never before.
For my beloved family, a pillar of strength,
For the challenges conquered, no length too great.

And oh, the friendships that bloomed and grew,
Like flowers in a garden, so vibrant and true.
Through laughter and tears, they stood by my side,
In the tapestry of life, a love that can't hide.

But now I stand at the edge of finality's door,
Where life's breath fades, and moments no more.
In the face of this truth, I find solace and grace,
For death, though final, leaves behind a trace.

For the memories cherished, the love that remains,
In the hearts of those left, where beauty sustains.
As I bid farewell to this earthly plane,
Know that my spirit lingers, forever ingrained.

So let the spring sunshine, let the city rejoice,
For life's journey ends, but love finds its voice.

In the legacy left, in the stories we share,
Death may be final, but love transcends there.

And as I depart, on this sunny spring day,
In the embrace of New York, my heart will stay.
Grateful for the blessings, the friendships so dear,
I face the finality, with a heart full of cheer.

FAREWELL

In the race of life, I've run my course,
With every step, I found my source,
Of solace and grace, a guiding light,
As I journeyed through day and night.

With every stride, I sought to find,
A purpose true, a peace of mind,
And as I crossed that finish line,
I knew my life had been divine.

For I leave behind a legacy,
A family woven in love's decree,
A tapestry of memories so grand,
A testament to a life well planned.

In the hearts of those I hold so dear,
My love and appreciation, crystal clear,
For they shared my journey, hand in hand,
Through joy and sorrow, they'd understand.

The laughter we shared, the tears we shed,
The moments of triumph, the dreams ahead,
All woven together, a symphony of life,
A testament to love's enduring strife.

And now, as I look back with pride,
At a life well lived, where love resides,
I find solace and grace in every breath,
Knowing I've left a legacy of love and depth.

For it's not wealth or worldly gain,
But the love we give, the joy we sustain,

That truly matters when all is said,
In the tapestry of a life well led.

So let the memories linger on,
In the hearts of those I've loved and known,
For in their souls, my spirit thrives,
As they carry forth the love that survives.

And as I bid farewell to this earthly plane,
I know my journey was not in vain,
For I leave behind a legacy so bright,
A life well lived, a beacon of light.

So let the world rejoice and sing,
For in my heart, love will forever cling,
To all those who shared my journey's worth,
I leave behind a legacy of love and mirth.

MY LEGACY

In the tapestry of life, may I impart,
A poem of the spirits, a gift from the heart,
For my loved ones to cherish, when I'm no longer near,
A reminder of the virtues that bring them cheer.

First, let love be the guiding light,
That shines through the darkness, so pure and bright,
May it bind their hearts with a sacred flame,
And fill their lives with an eternal claim.

Next, let patience be their steadfast guide,
As they navigate life's ebb and tide,
In moments of trial, may patience endure,
And bring them calmness, strong and sure.

Let joy dance in their souls, so free,
A symphony of laughter, pure and glee,
May it lift their spirits, in times of despair,
And remind them that happiness is always there.

Peace, a gentle river that soothes the soul,
A tranquil refuge, where serenity unfolds,
May it be their solace, a haven so serene,
As they navigate a world that can be mean.

Kindness, a beacon in a world so vast,
A gentle touch, a love that forever lasts,
May it be their compass, their guiding light,
As they spread compassion, both day and night.

Faithfulness, a bond that never breaks,
A promise kept no matter what it takes,

May it anchor their hearts in steadfast grace,
And strengthen their love in every embrace.

Gentleness, a touch that heals and mends,
A tender word, where empathy transcends,
May it be their armor, in a world so tough,
And bring them closer when times get rough.

Lastly, self-control, a virtue of might,
To temper desires, with wisdom's light,
May it guide their actions, with noble intent,
And lead them towards a life well-spent.

So, dear ones, may these gifts of the spirit,
Be your compass, as you journey through it,
And may my love forever reside,
In the pursuit of these virtues, side by side.

For when I'm gone, my spirit will be near,
Guiding your steps, calming your fear,
And in the legacy, I leave behind,
May these gifts of the spirit forever bind.

A TREASURE OF THE HEART

In the realm of cherished bonds, a friendship blooms,
A treasure of the heart, a gift that consumes.
Like a gentle breeze on a sunny day,
It brings solace and joy in its own special way.

With every passing moment, a friendship grows,
Through laughter and tears, it truly shows.
A shoulder to lean on, a listening ear,
A confidant and companion, always near.

In times of darkness, a friendship shines bright,
A beacon of hope, a guiding light.
Through life's ups and downs, it remains steadfast,
A source of strength, a bond that will last.

A precious friendship brings comfort and ease,
A sanctuary where hearts find peace.
With words unspoken, yet clearly understood,
It weaves a tapestry of love that's simply good.

In celebration or sorrow, a friend is there,
To offer support, to show they care.
With shared memories and stories to tell,
A friendship blossoms, a beautiful spell.

So let us cherish the gifts of a precious friendship,
For it is a blessing that knows no end ship.
With gratitude and love, our hearts will sing,
For a true friend is a priceless offering.

REALITY DISTORTION FIELD

In a realm of wonder, where dreams take hold,
Lies a phenomenon, a tale yet untold.
A reality distortion field, it's called,
Where possibilities flourish and unfold.

When humans unite with intent so strong,
And set a timeline, both short and long,
They conjure a force, like a magical wand,
Creating a path where success will throng.

Within this field, limits are erased,
Boundaries shattered, doubts effaced.
A goal is set, a vision embraced,
And the realm of possibility is embraced.

In this altered reality, minds collide,
Innovation blooms, like a rising tide.
With determination and passion inside,
The fruits of labor, they cannot hide.

New products emerge, born from the mind,
Bringing solutions, leaving no one behind.
With every hurdle, they persist and grind,
Creating a future that's one of a kind.

But beware, this field can deceive,
Blurring the line between fact and believe.
A cautionary tale, we must receive,
To stay grounded and not be naive.

So, harness this power, with caution and grace,
Embrace the challenges, at your own pace.

In the real distortion field, find your place,
And witness the miracles that you can chase.
For when humans create an intent so clear,
And set a time frame, without any fear,
The possibilities are endless, my dear,
In this reality distortion field, hold it near.

UNINTENDED CONSEQUENCES

Beware, dear dreamer, of the reality distortion field,
A realm where intentions and ambitions are revealed.
In this enchanting space, where dreams take flight,
Lies a cautionary tale, a warning of might.

For within this field, illusions abound,
Distorting perceptions, where truth may not be found.
As you shape your goals with fervent desire,
Take heed, for unintended consequences may transpire.

With every step forward, be cautious and wise,
For the line between reality and fiction may disguise.
The allure of achievement, so tempting and grand,
Can blind you to the perils that lie close at hand.

In this realm of distortion, time may slip away,
As the urgency of progress leads you astray.
Be mindful of the boundaries, don't lose sight,
Lest the consequences bring darkness to light.

The reality distortion field may breed obsession,
Where success becomes the sole possession.
But at what cost, dear dreamer, do you pursue?
Will it sacrifice the values that make you true?

Remember, dear dreamer, to stay grounded and aware,
To balance ambition with a mindful care.
For in the pursuit of goals, let integrity guide,
And let unintended consequences be cast aside.

So venture forth into the distortion with caution,
Embrace the possibilities with thoughtful action.

Let wisdom be your guide as you navigate,
The reality distortion field and its tempting state.

In this realm of dreams, where boundaries bend,
May your intentions and outcomes truly blend.
Learn from cautionary tales that came before,
And let your journey be one of growth and more.

YOUR GUIDING PRINCIPLES

When venturing through the reality distortion field,
Let guiding principles be your trusted shield.
Amidst the illusions and dreams that unfold,
Embrace what truly matters, let your heart be bold.

First, let truth be your compass, unwavering and true,
In this realm of distortion, let honesty shine through.
Seek the essence of reality, untainted and clear,
For integrity will guide you, banishing all fear.

Next, let wisdom be your companion, steady and wise,
Navigate the twists and turns with discerning eyes.
Make choices with prudence, consider every path,
For knowledge is power, safeguarding you from wrath.

Balance ambition with humility, my dear friend,
In this realm of dreams, let ego gently descend.
The pursuit of greatness should be fueled by grace,
For humility keeps you grounded in every space.

Kindness and compassion, let them be your light,
In the real distortion field, they'll shine so bright.
Extending a helping hand to others on the way,
For empathy and love bring harmony each day.

And amidst the chaos, hold onto your dreams,
Let passion be the fuel that ignites and redeems.
But remember, dear traveler, to stay true to your core,
Let your dreams align with the values you adore.

As you navigate the reality distortion field,
Let these guiding principles be your sturdy shield.

With truth, wisdom, humility, and love as your guide,
You'll transcend the illusions and reach the other side.

So, venture forth, my friend, with courage and grace,
Embrace the possibilities, let your dreams embrace.
For in this wondrous realm, where reality may sway,
Let your guiding principles light your path each day.

THE MATTHEW PRINCIPLE

In the realm of life, where dreams take flight,
There lies a principle, shining so bright.
It's called the Mathew principle, a guiding star,
A beacon of hope, no matter how far.

As you sow the seeds, in the fields of your quest,
The Mathew principle will put you to the test.
For it says, "To those who have, more shall be given,
But from those who have not, even the little will be taken."

It speaks of the power of momentum and growth,
Of how success builds upon success, both in breadth and both.
When you start with a little, and nurture it well,
The Mathew principle will weave its magic spell.

With every small victory, you'll gain confidence anew,
And the world will conspire to bring success to you.
For like a snowball rolling down a snowy hill,
The Mathew principle amplifies your skill.

But with great power comes the call for grace,
To use your success with humility, embrace.
For the Mathew principle reminds you, dear friend,
To share your blessings and kindness to no end.

It's not just about wealth or material gain,
The Mathew principle extends to every terrain.
In knowledge, in wisdom, in love, and in art,
It's about using your gifts to uplift every heart.

So embrace the Mathew principle, let it be your guide,

In all that you do, let its wisdom reside.
With each step forward, let growth be your aim,
And let generosity and humility be your flame.

For in the realm of life, where dreams take flight,
The Mathew principle shines with pure light.
Seize the opportunities that come your way,
And let the Mathew principle lead you each day.

MIND OVER MATTER

In the realm of possibilities, where dreams are born,
Lies a power within, waiting to be adorned.
It's the strength of the mind, the force that can shatter,
All barriers and doubts, for it's mind over matter.

When life throws its challenges, like a raging storm,
And it feels like the world is trying to deform,
Remember, my friend, you hold the key,
For the power of the mind can set you free.

With thoughts as your sword, and beliefs as your shield,
You can conquer mountains, make your dreams revealed.
For the mind is a canvas, where dreams come to play,
With imagination as the artist, painting your way.

When obstacles appear, like daunting walls to climb,
It's your mindset that determines the course of time.
For what may seem impossible, a mere illusion,
With a steadfast mind, becomes a grand fusion.

Through battles and struggles, you must persevere,
With determination and courage, conquer your fear.
For the mind is a warrior, relentless and strong,
It can turn weakness into triumph, right the wrong.

Believe in yourself, in the power you possess,
Harness your thoughts, it's the mind's finesse.
For when you control the thoughts that you think,
You'll realize that limits only exist at the brink.

So let your mind soar, like a bird in the sky,
Unfettered by doubts, let your spirit fly.

For the power of the mind knows no bounds,
It can create miracles, turn life around.

In the realm of possibilities, where dreams come true,
Remember, my friend, the power is in you.
With mind over matter, you'll conquer it all,
For the mind's strength is boundless, standing tall.

WALKING WITH DESTINY

In the journey of life, where paths intertwine,
There's a notion of destiny, a concept divine.
Walking hand in hand, with a purpose in sight,
We explore the depths of what feels right.

Destiny, my friend, is a compass of fate,
Guiding our steps, through choices we make.
It's the whisper in our hearts, the pull in our soul,
A force that nudges us towards our ultimate goal.

But what does it mean, to walk with destiny?
Is it preordained, or is it up to you and me?
Do we create our own reality, shape our own way?
Or are we merely puppets in a cosmic play?

Destiny is a dance, a partnership profound,
A collaboration of choices, both lost and found.
We're given opportunities, paths to explore,
But it's up to us to open the right door.

We have the power to create our own reality,
To shape our lives with intention and clarity.
For destiny is not a fixed destination in the sky,
But a tapestry we weave, as the days go by.

Through our thoughts and actions, we mold our fate,
Manifesting dreams, embracing love or hate.
The universe responds, to the energy we emit,
And our reality reflects the intentions we commit.

So walk with destiny, with courage and grace,
Embrace the challenges that life may embrace.

For in the depths of your heart, the truth will unfold,
That you hold the power to create a story untold.

Destiny is a journey, not a predetermined end,
It's the choices we make, the love we extend.
So let your footsteps be guided, by your heart's decree,
And create a reality, that sets your spirit free.

VICTORY

In the realm of dreams and aspirations so high,
There lies a path where victory draws nigh.
With every step taken, we inch closer each day,
Towards the life goals that we yearn to portray.

Victory, dear friend, is a flame that ignites,
A fire within us, pushing us to new heights.
It's the courage to rise, when faced with defeat,
And the strength to persevere, in moments bittersweet.

With unwavering determination, we forge ahead,
Embracing challenges, no matter how widespread.
For it's the journey that molds us, shapes our core,
And the lessons learned that make us soar.

In the face of adversity, we find our might,
Unyielding in our quest, to reach the light.
For victory lies not only in the final prize,
But in the growth and transformation that arise.

Each goal accomplished, a milestone to celebrate,
A testament to the dreams we passionately create.
With focus and discipline, we pave our way,
To a future where triumphs brightly display.

So let us move forward, with unwavering belief,
In our abilities, our purpose, and our inner relief.
For victory is not an end, but a continuous flow,
As we strive towards greatness and let our true selves grow.

Embrace the challenges, with a spirit unyielding,
And let passion guide us, our dreams revealing.

With victory as our companion, we'll conquer it all,
And stand tall, as we watch our life goals enthrall.

ARITHMETIC VS GEOMETRIC RETURN

In the realm of numbers, where patterns reside,
Two returns emerge, side by side.
Arithmetic and geometric, they stand apart,
Each with its own essence, in the realm of math's art.

Arithmetic return, steady and true,
A linear progression, tried and tested through.
With equal increments, it moves with grace,
A constant growth, in predictable space.

Geometric return, a different tale to tell,
Exponential growth, where wonders dwell.
Compounding power, it holds in its stride,
Multiplying wealth, as time continues to slide.

Arithmetic, a steady companion in finance,
A consistent gain, with a familiar dance.
It paints a picture of stability and ease,
A reliable path, where returns gently please.

Geometric, a force of exponential might,
A compounding miracle, soaring in flight.
It captures the essence of growth untamed,
Exponentially multiplying, as dreams are named.

In the realm of investments, they intertwine,
Calculations and strategies, aligning the divine.
Arithmetic provides a foundation strong,
While geometric amplifies, where profit belongs.

Both returns have their role, in the financial realm,
Navigating the numbers, to overwhelm.

Arithmetic brings balance, a steady hand,
While geometric propels, with a grand demand.

So let us embrace both, in harmony's embrace,
Understanding their differences, with grace.
For in the realm of returns, they dance and blend,
Creating a symphony where wealth knows no end.

WE ARE CREATORS
WITH A COSMIC FORCE

In the vast expanse of cosmic delight,
The truth emerges, shining so bright.
The universe, a tapestry of divine art,
Reflects our consciousness, a sacred part.

We are the creators, with power untold,
Within us, the universe's secrets unfold.
For deep within, our consciousness resides,
A cosmic force, where creation abides.

Every star that twinkles in the night,
Every planet that dances in cosmic light,
Every atom that weaves the fabric of space,
Reflects our consciousness, in grace.

With every thought, a ripple is born,
Expanding outward, the universe adorned.
Our dreams and desires, like shooting stars,
Manifesting galaxies, near and far.

The galaxies swirl in celestial dance,
Mirroring the depths of our conscious trance.
We are but stardust, connected and free,
Boundless creators, shaping our reality.

The mountains rise, majestic and grand,
Echoing the strength of our conscious hand.
The rivers flow, in harmony and flow,
Reflecting the peace within, as we grow.

The flowers bloom, in vibrant array,
Capturing the beauty of our thoughts each day.
The birds sing, a melody so sweet,
Harmonizing with our consciousness, complete.

In every breath, the universe breathes,
In every heartbeat, its rhythm perceives.
We are the vessels, through which it unfolds,
The universe and consciousness, forever enfolded.

So let us embrace this cosmic connection,
With gratitude and love, in every direction.
For we are the creators, the universe's song,
Consciousness in motion, forever strong.

KEEP DREAMING AND LEARNING

In the depths of existence, a purpose unfolds,
A journey of love, where life's story is told.
For within our hearts, a flame burns bright,
To experience love's embrace, day and night.

Life's purpose, a tapestry woven with care,
To cherish and share the love we bear.
In every smile, a connection is made,
A reminder that love will never fade.

Keep dreaming with eyes wide open,
For dreams are the whispers of a heart unbroken.
Through dreams, we explore new horizons afar,
Unleashing the magic that forever will spar.

Learning, the key to unlock boundless doors,
Expanding our minds, like never before.
In every lesson learned, growth is found,
Wisdom blossoms, a treasure profound.

Love, the essence that colors our days,
Guiding our steps through life's intricate maze.
To love and be loved, a gift so divine,
A symphony of hearts, in perfect rhyme.

In love's embrace, we find solace and peace,
A sanctuary where all worries cease.
Through love's lens, the world transforms,
A canvas of beauty, where our spirit warms.

So let us hold hands, and together we'll soar,
To heights unimagined, forevermore.

With hearts filled with love, dreams in our sight,
We'll learn, grow, and make every moment bright.

For the purpose of life is to experience love,
To keep dreaming and learning, guided from above.
In this grand tapestry, our souls intertwine,
Creating a legacy, timeless and divine.

LIFE'S SPLENDOR

Imagine a life where success knows no bounds,
Where dreams take flight, and purpose resounds.
Each step you take, a victory in its own right,
A symphony of accomplishments, shining so bright.

Picture a world filled with laughter and cheer,
As success dances around, drawing near.
The joy in your heart, like a radiant sun,
Illuminating the path, where triumph is won.

Visualize the moments of sheer delight,
As you conquer challenges with all your might.
The applause of triumph, echoing in the air,
A testament to your resilience and flair.

Imagine the feeling of reaching the top,
Where success and fulfillment never stop.
The taste of victory, so sweet on your lips,
As life's grand tapestry unfolds its bliss.

See yourself surrounded by loved ones so dear,
Sharing in the joy, with laughter and cheer.
For success is not measured in wealth alone,
But in the bonds of love that have grown.

Visualize a life where purpose aligns,
Where success and happiness intertwine.
A life of abundance, both inward and out,
Where dreams become reality, without a doubt.

In this vision of success, let your spirit soar,
Embrace the journey, forever wanting more.

For life's true splendor lies not in its end,
But in the pursuit of dreams, around the bend.

Dream big, my friend, and visualize with glee,
The life of success that awaits, for you to see.
With joy in your heart and a spirit so bright,
You'll bask in life's splendor, day and night.

TRANSFORMATIONAL EXPERIENCES

Expectations, like a compass, guide our way,
Igniting a fire within, come what may.
With belief in ourselves, we reach new heights,
Unleashing our talents, like dazzling lights.

But what makes an experience truly transforming,
That leaves an indelible mark, everlasting?
It's when we step outside our comfort zone,
Embracing the unknown, where growth is sown.

A transforming experience shakes us to the core,
Challenges our beliefs, and opens new doors.
It pushes us beyond our self-imposed limits,
And reveals hidden strengths, like radiant exhibits.

It can be a journey to a distant land,
Where cultures collide, and perspectives expand.
Immersed in diversity, we learn to embrace,
The beauty of differences, with love and grace.

Or perhaps it's a moment of profound loss,
That forces us to confront, without a gloss.
Through hardship and pain, we find resilience,
And emerge stronger, with newfound brilliance.

A transforming experience can be found,
In a simple act of kindness, so profound.
When we lend a helping hand to those in need,
Our hearts are touched, and souls are freed.

It can be a leap of faith, taking a chance,
To pursue a passion and join life's dance.

Stepping into the unknown with courage and trust,
We discover our purpose, turning dreams to dust.

In the depths of nature, we find solace and peace,
A transforming experience that brings us release.
From towering mountains to tranquil shores,
Nature's beauty transforms us to our core.

Seek out experiences that stir your soul,
That challenge inspire, and make you whole.
For it is through these transformative moments,
That we truly discover our purpose and essence.

A VISION SO BRIGHT

A transforming experience, a vision so bright,
Can illuminate your path, guide you through the night.
Living in a different country, a world anew,
Where cultures collide and dreams come true.

Immersed in the richness of unfamiliar lands,
You'll grow and evolve with open hands.
Adapting to customs, embracing diversity,
Expanding your horizons, with endless curiosity.

Studying a new language, a gateway unexplored,
Unveiling the beauty of words, like a roaring chord.
With each syllable learned, a connection is made,
Breaking down barriers, bridging the cascade.

Through the power of language, you'll find,
A deeper understanding of humankind.
Communicating with hearts, beyond words alone,
Transforming lives, with a linguistic tone.

And what of writing books, crafting stories untold,
Weaving words like silk, turning thoughts to gold.
In the realm of creation, ideas take flight,
Imprinting your essence, like stars in the night.

With each stroke of the pen, a world is born,
Characters dancing, emotions torn.
Sharing your voice with the world at large,
A transforming experience, like a guiding barge.

Bring clarity to your dreams, let them unfold,
Live in a different country, study languages bold.

Write books that inspire, that touch hearts and minds,
For it is through transformation, that true purpose finds.

Embrace the journey, step into the unknown,
With passion and courage, let your dreams be shown.
For when you're crystal clear about what you desire,
A transforming experience awaits, ready to inspire.

ASPIRE TO ACHIEVE GREATNESS

With **a** burning desire deep within my soul,
I yearn to make a difference, to reach my goal.
To be ready when opportunity knocks on my door,
And seize it with passion, forevermore.

I aspire to achieve greatness, to leave my mark,
To make ripples of positivity, even in the dark.
To forge my own trail, uncharted and new,
And in doing so, be authentically true.

For in this world, where conformity prevails,
I strive to be different, to set my sails.
To be profitably different, in every way,
And let my uniqueness shine, come what may.

Simplicity is the key, a guiding light,
To strip away the excess, and embrace what feels right.
To find beauty in the uncomplicated and pure,
And let it resonate, forever endure.

I seek to promote goodness, as my guiding star,
To uplift others, no matter how near or far.
To spread kindness, love, and compassion wide,
And make the world a better place, with every stride.

So, what am I uniquely qualified to do?
To promote something good, and see it through.
To desire deeply, and chase my dreams,
To embrace simplicity, and make it gleam.

I am ready to embrace the opportunities that come,
To shine my light, like the rising sun.

To be original, in all that I pursue,
And leave an indelible mark, that's uniquely true.

A PRELUDE TO SUCCESS

Failure, though daunting, can be reframed,
As a steppingstone to growth, where wisdom is gained.
It does not define us, nor make us less,
But fuels our resilience, our courage to progress.

With each stumble and fall, we are given a chance,
To choose our outcome, to rise and advance.
For success and failure, they dance hand in hand,
Compliments, not opposites, in life's grand plan.

Failure, you see, is a humble guide,
Providing feedback, with nothing to hide.
In depth lie lessons, waiting to be learned,
A prelude to success, where new paths are earned.

Let us embrace failure, with open arms,
For it unveils our strength, our hidden charms.
We learn to persevere, to adapt and grow,
To conquer new heights and let our spirits glow.

In the face of setbacks, we find our way,
We gather the pieces and start anew each day.
Failure becomes a catalyst, a force to ignite,
The fire within us, burning ever so bright.

So let us not fear failure, but welcome its grace,
For it shapes our character, at its own pace.
Success and failure, intertwined they remain,
Guiding us forward, in this intricate game.

With each failure, we rise, stronger than before,
With wisdom and courage, our hearts shall soar.

For failure, honorable, in its own right,
Is a stepping stone to success, shining so bright.

So let us embrace failure, and wear it with pride,
For it leads us to greatness, as we stride.
With every setback, we learn, we grow,
And success, like a phoenix, will surely show.

REFRAMING FAILURE

In the wake of a setback, when spirits are low,
There's solace in keeping busy, a way to let go.
For failure, my friend, can be reframed,
As a steppingstone to triumph, where success is ordained.

Keeping busy, we find solace and peace,
A distraction from failure, a balm to release.
In the midst of tasks and goals, we find our way,
Rebuilding our spirits, with each passing day.

Failure, you see, is not an end in itself,
But a chance to reflect, to reassess oneself.
It is a teacher, a guide on our path,
Molding our character, unveiling our strength.

Failure and success, they are intertwined,
Like the threads of a tapestry, perfectly aligned.
For success, without failure, holds little meaning,
It's the journey of setbacks that gives it its gleaming.

Failure is not a destination, nor a defeat,
But a lesson, feedback, for us to meet.
It's a catalyst for growth, a humble friend,
Guiding us forward, until success we transcend.

In relation to success, failure stands tall,
An integral part of the journey, for one and all.
It teaches resilience, and the power to rise,
To embrace challenges, with open eyes.

Failure reframed is a steppingstone,
A chance to rebuild, to stand on our own.

It shapes our character, strengthens our will,
And fuels our determination, with a fire that's still.

So, keep busy after a setback, my dear,
Let your actions drown out any lingering fear.
For failure, when reframed, paves the way,
To a future of success, brighter than the day.

LET CREATIVITY BLOOM

In the realm of creativity, where wonders unfold,
Lies the power to shape stories, both new and old.
For within the depths of our unconscious mind,
Lies the key to success and fulfillment, we find.

Imagination, a force that knows no bounds,
Unleashes the magic, where dreams can be found.
To feed our unconscious, we must let it roam,
In realms of inspiration, where ideas find their home.

To feed the unconscious, we must seek and explore,
New experiences, knowledge, and so much more.
Immerse in the arts, with colors, words, and sound,
Let curiosity guide us, to the treasures to be found.

Read books that inspire, that ignite the soul,
Let the pages transport us to places untold.
Listen to melodies, both gentle and bold,
That stirs emotions, and stories unfold.

Surround ourselves with beauty, in nature's embrace,
Let its wonders fuel us, with awe and grace.
Write, paint, create, with passion and might,
For through self-expression, we reach new heights.

Feed the unconscious with moments of stillness,
In silence and solitude, find inner brilliance.
Meditate, reflect, let thoughts gently flow,
As the unconscious whispers the seeds we sow.
Embrace the unknown, the risks, and the bets,
For in uncertainty, creativity begets.

And as life's story unfolds, with twists and turns,
Creativity guides us, as our spirit yearns.

Let us harness the power within,
To unlock the treasures, where dreams begin.
Feed the unconscious, let creativity bloom,
And success and self-fulfillment shall follow, in tune.

CHANGING YOUR REALITY

Imagine a future self of high achievement,
A version of you, with goals resplendent,
With passion and purpose, a driving force,
Creating a life where success is endorsed.

Embrace the journey, both bold and grand,
As you sculpt a future that's in your hand,
Let ambition guide you, with unwavering might,
And watch as your dreams come to life, in sight.

Work is no longer a burden to bear,
But a canvas for creativity, an opportunity rare,
Infuse passion and joy, in all that you do,
And watch as your talents shine through.

Make a difference in this world we share,
With kindness and compassion, show you care,
Whether big or small, your impact will spread,
Creating ripples of change, where hope is bred.

Find beauty in every moment, every day,
In the simplest of gestures, let kindness sway,
For in making a difference, we find our true worth,
And leave a legacy upon this Earth.

So, embrace the power within your soul,
To change your reality and make it whole,
Create a future self of high esteem,
Where work is fun and life is a dream.

Let your imagination soar, beyond the sky,
As you forge a path, where dreams never die,

And in the pursuit of your purpose and goals,
Discover the magic that lies within your soul.

For in changing your reality, you will find,
A life of fulfillment, of joy intertwined,
Creating a personality invention so true,
That reflects the greatness that resides in you.

Unreasonably success, a journey of delight,
Where dreams take flight, reaching new heights,
With the right attitude and strategies at hand,
We embrace the unknown, a fearless band.

So let us march forward, with hearts aflame,
Embracing the journey, never feeling tame,
For in unreasonably success, we find,
A life well-lived, a legacy designed.

BELIEVE IN YOUR ABILITIES

Embrace the power of intelligent determination,
A force that fuels your every aspiration,
With higher expectations, reach for the sky,
And watch as your dreams soar ever high.

Transforming experiences, lessons to learn,
Each challenge faced, a chance to discern,
The wisdom and strength that lies deep within,
As you navigate the journey, let resilience begin.

Believe in yourself, for you hold the key,
To unlock the doors of possibility,
With unwavering faith and confidence anew,
Success will be yours, in all that you do.

Surround yourself with those who inspire,
Whose passion and drive ignite your fire,
Together, you'll rise, reaching new heights,
Encouraging each other through days and nights.

In every setback, find a hidden treasure,
A lesson to learn, a chance for pleasure,
Adapt and grow, with a flexible mind,
Success is a journey, not a finish line.

Visualize your goals, with clarity and grace,
Envision the outcome, embrace the chase,
For the power of manifestation is strong,
As you align your actions, success will prolong.

With every step taken, let gratitude guide,
Appreciating the journey, the highs and the stride,

For success is not merely a destination,
But a state of being, a joyful revelation.

So, position yourself for success, my friend,
With positivity, strategies, and the will to transcend,
Believe in your abilities, let self-doubt cease,
And watch as your dreams become a masterpiece.

GAINING POWER
THROUGH MASTERMIND

In the realm of unreasonably success, behold,
A world where dreams come true, a story untold,
With the right attitude and strategies to employ,
We embark on a journey, filled with boundless joy.

In the realm of work and play, let us dance,
With hearts full of cheer, taking every chance,
For in the balance of both, we find our way,
Finding fulfillment in each passing day.

The forces of knowledge, a mighty tool,
To shape our path, to guide us through,
With each lesson learned, experience gained,
We grow and evolve, never feeling restrained.

Creative imagination, a gift to behold,
Unleashing ideas, stories yet untold,
In the realm of possibilities, we let our minds roam,
As we paint the canvas of life, creating our own home

Gaining power through the master mind,
A collective force, united and aligned,
Together we rise, lifting each other higher,
Harnessing the strength of our shared desire.

In the accumulation of experience, we find,
The wisdom and insights that shape our mind,
For every challenge faced, every hurdle crossed,
We gather strength, knowing we're not lost.

LIFE IS A PRECIOUS GIFT

In the morning's golden light, I rise,
Grateful for the gift of life that lies,
A precious treasure that I hold dear,
With each passing moment, it becomes clear.

The absolute best thing that came my way,
Was witnessing the sunrise, a glorious display,
Colors painted across the sky, a masterpiece,
Filling my heart with joy, a sense of inner peace.

And as I stood by the ocean's edge,
Listening to the waves, their rhythmic pledge,
A symphony of nature, a soothing sound,
Reminding me of life's wonders profound.

The refreshing breeze whispers in my ear,
A gentle reminder that all is well, nothing to fear,
I feel the presence of a higher power above,
The tall palm trees waving, a sign of love.

They tell me I am a child of God, so divine,
Guided and protected, my soul intertwines,
With the beauty of this world, so vast,
A reminder to seize each day, to make it last.

In this new day, I offer up my prayer,
For guidance to maximize blessings, to dare,
To live each moment with purpose and zest,
To embrace life's opportunities, to be my best.

For life is a precious gift, a fleeting chance,
To dance in the sunlight, to take a stance,

To cherish each sunrise, each ocean wave,
And in gratitude, my heart will forever crave.

So let us seize the day, with a joyful rhyme,
Carpe diem, embrace this precious time,
For in the beauty of life, we find our way,
A journey filled with blessings, day by day.

GOD'S LOVE

In the stillness of the night, I find solace,
As I listen to the whispers of divine grace,
The reassurance of God's love, so pure,
Filling my heart, making my spirit soar.

How precious I am in His sight,
A child embraced in His radiant light,
His words of love, like a gentle breeze,
Caressing my soul, putting my mind at ease.

I cherish the moments when I hear,
The comforting words that calm my fear,
Whispered softly in my listening ear,
A reminder of His presence, always near.

His love, like a river, flows endlessly,
Washing away doubts, setting my spirit free,
In His embrace, I find strength and peace,
A refuge in His love, a sweet release.

I am held in His arms, forever cherished,
His love for me, unwavering and unfaded,
His words, a symphony of tender care,
Guiding me through life, always there.

Oh, the refreshing words that I hold dear,
Whispering gently, banishing all my fears,
Reminding me of my worth, my value,
In His eyes, I am treasured, through and through.

I listen intently to His loving voice,
In every moment, I rejoice,

For His reassurance brings me peace,
A reminder that His love will never cease.

In the whispers of His love, I find my worth,
A precious soul, cherished from birth,
For in His words, I am truly blessed,
Forever embraced, in His love, I rest.

BELIEVE IN YOUR ABILITIES

Embrace the power of intelligent determination,
A force that fuels your every aspiration,
With higher expectations, reach for the sky,
And watch as your dreams soar ever high.

Transforming experiences, lessons to learn,
Each challenge faced, a chance to discern,
The wisdom and strength that lies deep within,
As you navigate the journey, let resilience begin.

Believe in yourself, for you hold the key,
To unlock the doors of possibility,
With unwavering faith and confidence anew,
Success will be yours, in all that you do.

Surround yourself with those who inspire,
Whose passion and drive ignite your fire,
Together, you'll rise, reaching new heights,
Encouraging each other through days and nights.

In every setback, find a hidden treasure,
A lesson to learn, a chance for pleasure,
Adapt and grow, with a flexible mind,
Success is a journey, not a finish line.

Visualize your goals, with clarity and grace,
Envision the outcome, embrace the chase,
For the power of manifestation is strong,
As you align your actions, success will prolong.

With every step taken, let gratitude guide,
Appreciating the journey, the highs and the stride,

For success is not merely a destination,
But a state of being, a joyful revelation.

So, position yourself for success, my friend,
With positivity, strategies, and the will to transcend,
Believe in your abilities, let self-doubt cease,
And watch as your dreams become a masterpiece.

GAINING POWER
THROUGH MASTERMIND

In the realm of unreasonably success, behold,
A world where dreams come true, a story untold,
With the right attitude and strategies to employ,
We embark on a journey, filled with boundless joy.

In the realm of work and play, let us dance,
With hearts full of cheer, taking every chance,
For in the balance of both, we find our way,
Finding fulfillment in each passing day.

The forces of knowledge, a mighty tool,
To shape our path, to guide us through,
With each lesson learned, experience gained,
We grow and evolve, never feeling restrained.

Creative imagination, a gift to behold,
Unleashing ideas, stories yet untold,
In the realm of possibilities, we let our minds roam,
As we paint the canvas of life, creating our own home.

Gaining power through the master mind,
A collective force, united and aligned,
Together we rise, lifting each other higher,
Harnessing the strength of our shared desire.

In the accumulation of experience, we find,
The wisdom and insights that shape our mind,
For every challenge faced, every hurdle crossed,
We gather strength, knowing we're not lost.

Unreasonably success, a journey of delight,
Where dreams take flight, reaching new heights,
With the right attitude and strategies at hand,
We embrace the unknown, a fearless band.

So let us march forward, with hearts aflame,
Embracing the journey, never feeling tame,
For in unreasonably success, we find,
A life well-lived, a legacy designed.

LIFE IS A PRECIOUS GIFT

In the morning's golden light, I rise,
Grateful for the gift of life that lies,
A precious treasure that I hold dear,
With each passing moment, it becomes clear.

The absolute best thing that came my way,
Was witnessing the sunrise, a glorious display,
Colors painted across the sky, a masterpiece,
Filling my heart with joy, a sense of inner peace.

And as I stood by the ocean's edge,
Listening to the waves, their rhythmic pledge,
A symphony of nature, a soothing sound,
Reminding me of life's wonders profound.

The refreshing breeze whispers in my ear,
A gentle reminder that all is well, nothing to fear,
I feel the presence of a higher power above,
The tall palm trees waving, a sign of love.

They tell me I am a child of God, so divine,
Guided and protected, my soul intertwines,
With the beauty of this world, so vast,
A reminder to seize each day, to make it last.

In this new day, I offer up my prayer,
For guidance to maximize blessings, to dare,
To live each moment with purpose and zest,
To embrace life's opportunities, to be my best.

For life is a precious gift, a fleeting chance,
To dance in the sunlight, to take a stance,

To cherish each sunrise, each ocean wave,
And in gratitude, my heart will forever crave.

So let us seize the day, with a joyful rhyme,
Carpe diem, embrace this precious time,
For in the beauty of life, we find our way,
A journey filled with blessings, day by day.

GOD'S LOVE

In the stillness of the night, I find solace,
As I listen to the whispers of divine grace,
The reassurance of God's love, so pure,
Filling my heart, making my spirit soar.

How precious I am in His sight,
A child embraced in His radiant light,
His words of love, like a gentle breeze,
Caressing my soul, putting my mind at ease.

I cherish the moments when I hear,
The comforting words that calm my fear,
Whispered softly in my listening ear,
A reminder of His presence, always near.

His love, like a river, flows endlessly,
Washing away doubts, setting my spirit free,
In His embrace, I find strength and peace,
A refuge in His love, a sweet release.

I am held in His arms, forever cherished,
His love for me, unwavering and unfaded,
His words, a symphony of tender care,
Guiding me through life, always there.

Oh, the refreshing words that I hold dear,
Whispering gently, banishing all my fears,
Reminding me of my worth, my value,
In His eyes, I am treasured, through and through.

I listen intently to His loving voice,
In every moment, I rejoice,

For His reassurance brings me peace,
A reminder that His love will never cease.

In the whispers of His love, I find my worth,
A precious soul, cherished from birth,
For in His words, I am truly blessed,
Forever embraced, in His love, I rest.

ALLIANCE WITH GREAT MINDS

In the realm of dreams and innovation's embrace,
I ponder the significance of alliance, with grace,
Great minds that have shaped our world's course,
Ford, Edison and Burroughs with their creative force.

Oh, the importance of joining hands with these minds,
Whose brilliance and wisdom forever shines,
They paved the way for progress and change,
Their alliance, a catalyst for a new range.

Henry Ford, the visionary of the assembly line,
Revolutionizing industry, a concept so fine,
His partnership with innovation, a driving force,
Transformed the world, steering a new course.

Thomas Edison, the wizard of invention,
With his alliance, sparked a revolution,
Lighting up the world with the incandescent glow,
His brilliance, a beacon for all to follow.

John Burroughs, the naturalist and sage,
Through his alliance, he ignited wonder and engage,
Exploring the depths of nature's grand design,
His words inspiring, like a poetry divine.

In alliance with these great minds, we find,
A synergy of ideas, a collective bind,
Their wisdom and expertise, a guiding light,
Igniting the flame of innovation, burning bright.

For in alliance, we transcend our own limitations,
We amplify our impact, our aspirations,

Sharing knowledge, insights, and passion,
We forge a path towards progress and compassion.

So let us seek alliance with these great souls,
Embracing their wisdom, as our journey unfolds,
For in their minds, lies a treasure trove,
A testament to the power of alliance, we shall prove.

In the company of Henry Ford, Thomas Edison,
John Burroughs, and those who have risen,
We find inspiration, courage, and might,
To create a future that shines oh so bright.

In alliance with great minds, we shall stand,
Hand in hand, united, we'll expand,
The boundaries of what is known and seen,
Together, we'll shape a world, evergreen.

OUR HUMAN EMOTIONS

In the tapestry of human endeavor and strife,
We find the influence of the emotion of sex, rife,
For it intertwines with our deepest desires,
Igniting flames of passion and inspiring fires.

Men and women of great achievements, we see,
Driven by the allure of intimacy's plea,
The power of attraction, a force untamed,
Fuels their actions, leaving their mark untamed.

Love, a potent elixir that binds and entwines,
Has shaped the path of many brilliant minds,
From poets who penned verses of devotion,
To artists who captured love's graceful motion.

Fame, a seductive mistress, tempts and charms,
Inspiring ambition to reach for the stars,
Driven by the desire to be known and adored,
Many have achieved greatness, their names soared.

Power, an intoxicating elixir, it holds,
Influencing minds and stories yet untold,
Driven by the hunger for control and might,
Leaders have emerged, shaping history's flight.

Music, a language that speaks to the soul,
Conveying emotions beyond words' control,
Through melodies and rhythms, it captivates,
Inspiring greatness in those it permeates.

Harmony, the essence of balance and peace,
Influencing minds to strive for release,

The quest for unity, a driving force,
Bringing together nations, forging a course.

The emotions that stir within our hearts,
Shape our actions, igniting life's vibrant arts,
Sex, love, fame, power, music, and harmony,
They intertwine, shaping our humanity.

So let us embrace these emotions with care,
Harnessing their power, aware and aware,
For within their realm lies both light and dark,
A force that can ignite or leave a lasting mark.

May we, as humans, be guided by the light,
Using these emotions to elevate and unite,
Inspiring greatness, compassion, and grace,
Leaving a legacy of love in every space.

LOVE ENDLESS POWER

In the realm of brilliance, where minds do roam,
Love's gentle touch has found a cherished home.
For in the depths of passion's sacred fire,
Brilliant minds are shaped and inspired.

Love, the muse that sparks creative flame,
Ignites the minds of artists without shame.
From poets who weave words with tender grace,
To painters who capture love's radiant face.

In the hearts of thinkers, philosophers wise,
Love's influence becomes their greatest prize.
For in the embrace of affection's sweet hold,
Ideas flourish; stories unfold.

The scientist, with love's curiosity,
Explores the mysteries of life's tapestry.
Driven by the desire to understand,
Love guides their quest, hand in hand.

Musicians, composers, their hearts alight,
Compose symphonies that touch souls at night.
For love's melody, a universal song,
Inspires them to create, to belong.

Love's influence on brilliant minds is vast,
It shapes their thoughts, their visions steadfast.
From mathematicians to scholar's profound,
Love's essence in their work is found.

For love, the force that binds and connects,
Inspires brilliance, fuels intellect.

In the presence of love's tender grace,
Brilliant minds find their destined place.

So let us celebrate love's endless power,
As it influences minds, hour after hour.
For in the embrace of love's gentle sway,
Brilliance blossoms, lighting the way.

SOURCES OF WISDOM

In the realm of knowledge, where wisdom dwells,
There lie the sources, where understanding swells.
From ancient times to the present day,
Let's explore the pathways where knowledge lay.

The first source, a spark of divine creation,
Is the genius within, igniting imagination.
Through six senses, we perceive the world around,
The touch, taste, smell, sight, sound, and profound.

Next, the infinite intelligence, deep and vast,
Resides within us, a treasure unsurpassed.
Our subconscious mind, a realm untold,
Where insights and wisdom forever unfold.

And in the mystery of the river and the stream,
Lies a source of knowledge, like a waking dream.
The currents of life, flowing ceaselessly,
Carrying insights, lessons, and clarity.

Books and writings, the written word,
Are sources of knowledge, often unheard.
From ancient scriptures to modern prose,
They guide us on the paths that wisdom shows.

Nature, a teacher of profound grace,
Reveals its secrets in every embrace.
From the whispering trees to the roaring sea,
Its vastness and beauty, a source for us to see.

The wise and learned, their minds refined,
Are sources of knowledge, endlessly kind.

Their wisdom shared, like a guiding light,
Illuminating our path, with knowledge bright.

And lastly, in the depths of introspection,
Lies a source of knowledge, our own reflection.
Through self-discovery, we learn and grow,
Unveiling truths that only we can know.

So let us seek knowledge from these fountains,
Expand our minds, climb limitless mountains.
For in the sources of wisdom and insight,
We find the keys to knowledge's endless flight.

THE DRIVEN POWER OF SEX

Personal magnetism, a captivating spell,
From the exchange handshake to posture that tells.
The way we carry ourselves, with grace and poise,
Attraction radiates, like a melody's voice.

The vibration of thoughts, an unseen force,
Sending ripples through souls, with its magnetic course.
Positive or negative, they hold immense might,
Shaping perceptions, like stars in the night.

Body appearance, a canvas to express,
The essence is within, a captivating dress.
From eyes that sparkle, to smiles that gleam,
Beauty unfolds, like a mesmerizing dream.

And in the realm of sex energy's embrace,
Passions ignite, like a fiery blaze.
A primal drive, connecting hearts and souls,
Unveiling desires, that only intimacy knows.

But amidst the influences that feelings bring,
Let not falter, let not wisdom cling.
For while emotions guide, they can also deceive,
To find true balance, we must perceive.

Let us navigate the currents of desire,
With self-awareness and a heart on fire.
Harnessing the power, but not losing sight,
Of the deeper truths that make our souls ignite.

For in the realm of human connection's sway,
We find the essence of our own display.

Feelings may guide, but it's our choices that define,
The path we walk, the love we intertwine.

So let us honor the power of emotions' sway,
But with discernment, let us find our way.
For in the tapestry of life's intricate art,
We are the weavers, shaping love's sacred part.

IGNITING THE FLAME OF PROGRESS

Throughout history, there have been women who inspired,
Igniting the flame of progress, setting minds on fire.
Their achievements, like stars in the sky,
Illuminate the path for all to try.

Take Marie Curie, a pioneer of science's realm,
Her discoveries, like a radiant helm.
Inspired by her love, Pierre's unwavering support,
Together they unlocked secrets, science's fort.

Or Ada Lovelace, a visionary mind,
Her work with Charles Babbage, one of a kind.
The first computer programmer, she paved the way,
For the digital age we embrace today.

In the arts, too, women have shone,
Their creativity and talent widely known.
Emily Dickinson, with her introspective verse,
Unveiled the human soul, in each line immersed.

And let us not forget Rosa Parks, a woman of might,
Whose act of defiance sparked a civil rights fight.
Her refusal to give up her seat on the bus,
Inspired a movement, reminding us of justice.

These are just a few examples, a glimpse in time,
Of women who've inspired, their achievements sublime.
In this time and space reality, their voices are heard,
Their contributions acknowledged, their legacies preserved.

So let us celebrate this moment so bright,
Where women's achievements shine with all their might.

For in their footsteps, we find inspiration anew,
And together, we'll build a world that is true.

WOMEN IN SCIENCE
AND TECHNOLOGY

In the realm of science and technology's domain,
Women have left an indelible stain.
Their brilliance and passion, a guiding light,
Leading us forward with relentless might.

Marie Curie, a name forever revered,
Her pioneering work, we hold so dear.
With her discovery of radioactivity's power,
She unraveled the secrets of atoms, hour by hour

Rosalind Franklin's X-ray diffraction,
Unveiled the structure of DNA in action.
Her crucial findings, though often overlooked,
Laid the foundation for genetic breakthroughs.

Hedy Lamarr, a star of the silver screen,
Had a mind that was sharp and keen.
Her invention of frequency hopping, a marvel indeed,
Paved the way for modern wireless technology's lead.

Grace Hopper, a visionary in computing's sphere,
Developed the first compiler, a breakthrough so clear.
Her work on programming languages, a gift,
Make computers more accessible, giving us a lift.

Chien-Shiung Wu, a physicist of great acclaim,
Unraveled the mysteries of weak force's game.
Her experiments shattered established beliefs,
Confirming parity violation, a discovery beyond belief.

These women, and countless others unnamed,
Have left an imprint that cannot be tamed.
Their contributions to science and technology,
We have shaped our world with profound efficacy.

So let us honor their brilliance and might,
And strive to empower the women in sight.
For they hold the key to innovation's door,
And together, we'll forge a future worth fighting for.

WOMEN IN THE ARTS

In the realm of arts, where imagination thrives,
Women have left a mark, their talent survives.
Their creativity and passion, a radiant flame,
Illuminating the world with their artistic acclaim.

Frida Kahlo, a painter with a vibrant soul,
Her self-portraits spoke, emotions unrolled.
Through her brush, she bared her pain and strife,
Creating masterpieces that captured life.

Maya Angelou, a poet of profound grace,
Her words danced on paper, leaving a lasting trace.
With her powerful verses, she gave voice,
To the struggles and triumphs, a poetic choice.

Georgia O'Keeffe, a painter of exquisite blooms,
Her floral canvases were like nature's heirlooms.
With her bold strokes, she unveiled the unseen,
Celebrating beauty, both fierce and serene.

Nina Simone, a voice that stirred the soul,
Her melodies held power, making hearts whole.
Through her music, she fought for rights and peace,
A songbird of justice, her legacy won't cease.

Audrey Hepburn, an actress with elegance untold,
Her presence on screen, a story unfold.
With grace and charm, she captivated all,
Leaving an indelible mark, standing tall.

These women, and many more yet to be named,
Have enriched the arts, their impact acclaimed.

Their contributions have shaped our cultural core,
And inspired generations forevermore.

So let us celebrate their artistic might,
And honor the women who shine so bright.
For their creativity knows no bounds,
And together, we'll create a world where art resounds.

A CHAMPION FOR WOMEN'S RIGHTS

In the realm of colors, where dreams take flight,
A free spirit emerged, shining so bright.
Frida Kahlo, a woman of strength and grace,
Left an indelible mark, a timeless embrace.

With paintbrush in hand, she painted her soul,
Expressing her truth, making it whole.
Through vibrant strokes, she unveiled her pain,
A visual diary, a window to her inner terrain.

Her self-portraits spoke of resilience and strife,
A mirror reflecting the complexities of life.
In each stroke, a story, a chapter untold,
Her art became a voice, a tale to behold.

Frida, a symbol of empowerment and pride,
Inspiring women to break free and stride.
Her unapologetic spirit, a beacon of light,
Guiding us through darkness, igniting our fight.

She embraced her uniqueness, her flaws unmasked,
Challenging conventions, her spirit steadfast.
Her unibrow and colorful attire,
A defiance of norms, a symbol to inspire.

Frida, a champion for women's rights,
A voice for the silenced, shining her light.
She shattered confines, stood against the tide,
Empowering women worldwide to rise and stride.

Her legacy lives on, her influence profound,
Her art and spirit continue to astound.

Frida Kahlo, a muse for the ages,
A symbol of courage, defying life's cages.

So let us celebrate her free-spirited soul,
Her contributions to women, making us whole.
May her art and legacy forever endure,
Inspiring generations, forever pure.

WOMEN IN THE STEM FIELD

In the realm of knowledge, where discoveries unfold,
Women have left their mark, their stories untold.
In science, technology, engineering, and math,
Their contributions have paved a mighty path.

From the stars above to the depths of the sea,
Women have explored with curiosity.
In labs and workshops, their brilliance shines,
Breaking barriers, reaching new horizons.

Marie Curie, a pioneer of radiance,
Unveiling the secrets of atomic substance.
Her research on radiation, a breakthrough so grand,
A Nobel laureate, an inspiration to withstand.

Ada Lovelace, a visionary mind,
In the world of computing, she was defined.
Her analytical engine is so vast,
Laying the foundation for the digital contrast.

Katherine Johnson, a mathematician so bright,
Calculating trajectories, guiding flights.
Her calculations, a vital key,
Space exploration's remarkable decree.

Rosalind Franklin, a DNA pioneer,
Unraveling the structure, so crystal clear.
Her X-ray images, a glimpse into life's code,
A crucial contribution, forever bestowed.

Mae Jemison, an astronaut of grace,
Soaring beyond limits, conquering space.

Her journey to the stars, an inspiration profound,
Breaking barriers and stereotypes abound.

Women worldwide, in labs and fields,
Their contributions, an endless yield.
From breakthroughs in medicine to technological leaps,
Their brilliance and innovation forever keeps.

For every woman who dared to pursue,
A path less traveled, dreams pursued,
We celebrate your courage, your intellect so vast,
In science, technology, engineering, and math.

May the world recognize your significant role,
Your brilliance, your spirit, your eternal soul.
As you continue to shape a future so bright,
May your contributions be forever in sight.

WOMEN IN EDUCATION

In the realm of education, where minds ignite,
Women have championed learning with all their might.
Their contributions, like beacons in the night,
Illuminate the path to knowledge, shining bright.

Maria Montessori, a pioneer of education,
Her method empowered children, a revelation.
With hands-on learning and freedom to explore,
She nurtured young minds, forevermore.

Helen Keller, a symbol of resilience and grace,
Her pursuit of education, a remarkable embrace.
Despite her challenges, she soared above,
Inspiring others with her boundless love.

Malala Yousafzai, a voice for girls' education,
Her bravery and advocacy, a global sensation.
Defying oppression, she fought for the right,
To educate every girl, with all her might.

Anne Sullivan, a teacher of profound impact,
Her dedication to Helen Keller, a profound pact.
With patience and perseverance, she taught,
Opening doors of knowledge, with lessons fraught.

Dr. Maria Montessori, a visionary in her reign,
Her educational philosophy, a transformative gain.
With child-centered learning and freedom to explore,
She empowered young minds, forevermore.

Mary McLeod Bethune, an educational trailblazer,
Her commitment to African American students

With the founding of Bethune-Cookman University,
She created opportunities, breaking barriers with unity.

Dorothy Vaughan, a mathematician of remarkable skill,
Her leadership at NASA, a story to thrill.
As a teacher and mentor, she paved the way,
For women in STEM, to shine every day.

These women, and countless more,
Have left an indelible mark, forever to adore.
In the field of education, their voices resound,
Guiding generations, lifting knowledge profound.

Their contributions, a testament to their might,
Inspiring learners, igniting sparks so bright.
To all the women in education, we celebrate your grace,
Your dedication and wisdom, the world does embrace.

So let us honor their achievements, let us proclaim,
The incredible contributions of women in education's do-
main.
For their passion and commitment, their love and drive,
Have shaped a world where minds thrive.

WOMEN'S HEALTH

In the realm of women's health, where care is sought,
Women have made contributions, far and thought.
Their dedication and expertise, a steadfast support,
Empowering women, their well-being to exhort.

Florence Nightingale, a trailblazer in nursing,
Her tireless work, compassion so nurturing.
In the midst of war, she brought healing's light,
Pioneering modern nursing, shining ever so bright.

Dr. Elizabeth Blackwell, a medical pioneer,
Her determination broke barriers so severe.
As the first female doctor, she blazed a trail,
Opening doors for women, without fail.

Dr. Rebecca Lee Crumpler, a physician of acclaim,
The first African American woman to attain the same.
Her compassion and skill, a beacon of care,
Uplifting the health of women everywhere.

Dr. Virginia Apgar, an advocate for newborns,
Her Apgar score, saving lives by the cords.
Ensuring the health of babies, right from the start,
Her contribution to obstetrics, a work of art.

Dr. Helen Brooke Taussig, a pioneer in cardiology,
Her expertise in pediatric heart surgery,
Transformed the lives of countless children,
With her dedication, love, and precision.

Margaret Sanger, a champion of women's rights,
Her fight for birth control, breaking societal fights.

Empowering women to make choices so profound,
Her legacy in reproductive health, forever renowned.

Dr. Jane Goodall, a primatologist and conservationist,
Her research on chimpanzees, a breakthrough amidst.
Promoting the importance of animal health,
And its connection to human well-being, with stealth.

These women, and many more in the field,
Have advanced women's health, their work revealed.
With passion and expertise, they've made a mark,
Improving lives and creating a lasting spark.

Their contributions, a testament to their might,
Advocating for women's health, shining so bright.
To all the women in the realm of care,
We celebrate your compassion, beyond compare.

So let us honor their achievements, let us proclaim,
The incredible contributions of women in health's domain.
For their dedication and wisdom, the world does embrace,
Empowering women, ensuring their well-being finds grace.

In the realm of women's health, their legacy stands,
Guiding generations with caring hands.
Their contributions, a beacon of hope,
Inspiring women to thrive and cope.

LIFE'S CREATION

In the realm of life's creation, a wondrous sight,
Women hold a power, a gift of pure light.
Their bodies, a vessel, where life begins,
A miracle unfolding, as a new chapter begins.

In the embrace of motherhood, women find,
A connection to the universe, so divine.
For in their womb, a tiny heartbeat thrives,
A testament to the miracle of human lives.

From the first flutter of life, tender and small,
To the kicks and movements, a dance in the hall,
Women nurture and protect, with every breath,
Creating a haven, shielding life from death.

With each passing day, a bond does grow,
Between mother and child, a love that does flow.
Through ups and downs, joys and tears,
A mother's love, eternal and fierce.

But let us not forget, in this journey profound,
The role of men, their support so renowned.
For fathers stand strong, alongside their wives,
Creating a foundation, where love truly thrives.

Together they navigate the unknown,
Through the challenges faced, they have grown.
With love and dedication, they pave the way,
For a future filled with hope, each and every day.

So let us honor the women, whose bodies give,
The gift of life, so precious, so vivid.

Their ability to create, to nurture and bear,
A testament to the strength that they wear.

And let us also honor the men, their contribution,
To the creation of life, a vital solution.
For in their love and support, they provide,
The foundation for a family to thrive.

In the realm of women's health and childbearing,
We celebrate the miracle of life, so endearing.
For it is through their unique ability to conceive,
That human beings continue to flourish and believe.

So let us cherish the women, the mothers so dear,
Their strength and resilience, forever near.
And let us acknowledge the men, the fathers so true,
For their love and support, in all that they do.

For in the celebration of life's creation,
We honor the bond that defies explanation.
The unity of women and men, a harmonious blend,
Continuing the human story, from beginning to end.

LET YOUR IMAGINATION TAKE FLIGHT

In a world where possibilities abound,
Breakthroughs are not for the brightest or strongest, I've found.
They are reserved for those who dare to dream,
For those who believe in a different way, it may seem.

Are you ready to embark on a journey anew?
To explore uncharted paths, to dare to pursue,
A vision that lies beyond the realm of the known,
Where breakthroughs await, patiently sown.

For when you dare to dream, with eyes wide open,
The universe conspires, with wonders unbroken.
Opportunities present themselves, in subtle ways,
As if beckoning you to step into the maze.

Breakthroughs are not confined to a chosen few,
They're available to all, to me and to you.
It's not about intelligence or physical might,
But about the courage to envision a different light.

So let your imagination take flight,
Embrace the unknown, with all your might.
For in the realm of dreams, there lies the key,
To unlock the doors of possibility.

With every step you take towards the unknown,
Breakthroughs await, seeds of change to be sown.
Embrace the challenges, the twists and turns,
For it is through them, that wisdom is earned.

Dare to dream of a different way,
And watch as breakthroughs grace your day.
For when you believe in the power within,
Miracles unfold as the journey begins.

So, are you ready to dare to dream?
To embrace the extraordinary, as it may seem?
Breakthroughs are available, just a step away,
When you dare to dream, every single day.

LIFE'S EBB AND FLOW

In life's ebb and flow, we find the beauty,
A dance of moments, both high and low.
With each rise and fall, we must adapt,
Embrace the change and never be trapped.

Like a river that flows through rugged terrain,
Life takes us on a journey, never the same.
The currents may shift, the path may twist,
But it's in our nature to persist.

For in the face of challenges we grow,
It's through adversity that strength will show.
Like a seed that sprouts in the harshest of soil,
We too can flourish, through effort and toil.
So let us evolve, like the seasons that change,
Embracing new chapters, embracing the strange.
For stagnation breeds only discontent,
But growth and learning bring fulfillment.

As we navigate the ebbs and flows of life,
Let us remember the importance of strife.
For it's through challenges we truly know,
The power to adapt, evolve, and grow.

So let us dance with the rhythm of time,
Embracing each moment, both sublime and sublime.
For life's ebb and flow is a precious gift,
And it's in our journey, our spirits lift.

THE SEASONS OF OUR LIFE

In the tapestry of life, seasons unfold,
Each brings a story, both new and old.
From the vibrant bloom of spring's gentle embrace,
To the fiery colors of autumn's grace.

As the seasons change, so must we,
Adapting and evolving, like a mighty tree.
For life's journey is a constant flow,
And in every season, we must grow.

In the spring of our youth, we blossom and bloom,
Exploring the world, chasing dreams in full bloom.
Opportunities abound, like flowers in bloom,
We seize them with vigor, our spirits in tune.

But as summer arrives, the heat of life's quest,
We face challenges and put ourselves to the test.
Yet amidst the trials, we find strength and resilience,
And learn the power of perseverance.

Autumn comes with colors, vibrant and bold,
A reminder that change is a story untold.
We let go of what no longer serves our soul,
Embracing new beginnings, letting our hearts unfold.

And finally, winter arrives, a season of rest,
A time to reflect, to nurture and invest.
In the stillness, we discover our true desires,
And ignite the fire within, rekindling our fires.

Through every season, we must keep moving ahead,
Embrace the unknown, where opportunities spread.

For in change and growth, we find our true worth,
And create a life of purpose and mirth.

So let us welcome the seasons of life,
With open arms and hearts, free from strife.
Adapt, evolve, grow, keep moving forward,
For each season, our spirits are restored.

LIFE'S TRANSITIONS

In the race of life, with others we may compare,
But the true victory lies in running our own affair.
For each of us carries a unique flame inside,
Talent, a passion, that sets us apart with pride.

In this journey of transitions, when paths diverge,
We must remember, it's our own race to surge.
Opportunities lie hidden, waiting to be found,
If we keep our mindset strong, our actions profound.

No need to follow in the footsteps of another,
For our own abilities, we must uncover.
Embrace your talents, let them shine bright,
For in your authenticity, you'll find true delight.

In times of change, uncertainty may prevail,
But let not fear or doubt make you derail.
Trust in yourself, in your strength and grace,
And navigate the transitions at your own pace.

The road may be winding, with twists and turns,
But in these moments, true growth discerns.
Each transition a chance, a door to explore,
To learn, to evolve, and to open new doors.

Remember, it's not about the destination alone,
But the journey, the lessons, the seeds we've sown.
Run your own race, with passion and zeal,
And let your unique talents be the real deal.

So, seek opportunities in life's transitions,
With a mindset focused on positive visions.

Take care of your actions, nurture your soul,
And let your own race be your ultimate goal.

For in running our own race, we find true bliss,
In embracing our talents, our purpose we kiss.
So, run with conviction, and seize every chance,
For in living authentically, your life will dance.

A FAREWELL,
A CELEBRATION OF LIFE

In a moment of loss, when tears may fall,
Let's create a celebration, a joyous call.
For a funeral can be more than just sorrow and pain,
It can be a tribute, a memory, a beautiful refrain.

Let's gather together, with hearts open wide,
To honor a life with love as our guide.
Instead of mourning, let's celebrate and share,
The precious moments, the memories we bear.

In this arrangement of farewell, let's paint with bright hues,
With flowers of joy, and laughter infused.
Let's choose vibrant colors, like a rainbow's embrace,
To symbolize a life lived with passion and grace.

In place of tears, let's share stories and tales,
Of moments cherished, of love that prevails.
Let's celebrate the laughter, the shared delight,
And remember the joy that made their days bright.

Let's fill the room with music, with melodies sweet,
That uplifts the spirit and make hearts skip a beat.
For music has a way, to heal and transcend,
To bring comfort and solace, to help hearts mend.

Let's create an atmosphere of warmth and love,
With candles aglow, like stars up above.
A gentle ambiance, that soothes and consoles,
As we honor a life that touched many souls.

Let's invite laughter, let it fill the air,
For in laughter, we find strength to bear.
Let's share anecdotes, the funny and absurd,
And celebrate the moments that brought smiles and stirred.

And as we bid farewell, let's release our grief,
With balloons that soar high, offering relief.
Each balloon is a symbol of love that remains,
Elevating spirits, easing our pains.

So, let's create a celebration, a farewell so grand,
Where sadness and sorrow can no longer stand.
For in celebrating a life, we find solace and peace,
And honor the legacy that will never cease.

Let's remember the love, the joy, and the light,
And celebrate a life that shone ever so bright.
In this celebration of life, let's find our way,
To cherish the memories, each and every day.

LET'S HONOR THEIR JOURNEY

In the realm of farewells, where hearts are tender,
A celebration of life, a tribute to render.
With music as our guide, and balloons above,
Let's honor their journey with boundless love.

As melodies float through the air so sweet,
Each note is a memory, a moment to greet.
The rhythm of life, the harmony of souls,
Through music's embrace, our sorrow consoles.

And balloons, oh balloons, they dance in the sky,
Symbols of freedom, as they rise up high.
In colors so vibrant, they carry our dreams,
A message of hope, as life's tapestry gleams.

The red balloon, a symbol of courage and might,
For a life lived boldly, in the face of every fight.
It soars with determination, defying all odds,
A testament to strength, as we applaud.

The blue balloon, a symbol of peace and calm,
Reflecting the serenity, like a soothing balm.
It whispers of tranquility, in moments of despair,
Guiding us gently, with love beyond compare.

The yellow balloon, a symbol of joy and cheer,
Reminding us to smile, even through tears.
It radiates sunshine, a warmth that won't fade,
A celebration of laughter, the memories we've made.

The pink balloon, a symbol of love's embrace,
A tender reminder, in this sacred space.

It carries affection, in every gentle sway,
A testament to the love that will never decay.

And as the balloons ascend, higher and higher,
They carry our wishes, our love, and desire.
They reach for the heavens, where spirits reside,
A farewell, a celebration, with love as our guide.

So let the music play, let the balloons take flight,
As we gather in unity, to honor the light.
In this celebration of life, let our spirits unite,
As we bid farewell, with love shining bright.

For in the music and balloons, we find solace and peace,
A tribute to a life that will never cease.
So let us remember, the laughter, the tears,
In this celebration, love perseveres.

THE MAN OF TODAY

The man of today, with his mind so bright,
Embarks on a journey, seeking truth and light.
He breaks the chains that bound his soul,
Embracing progress, as generations unfold.

No longer confined to the roles of the past,
He breaks the barriers, with determination vast.
He seeks equality, in every aspect of life,
Empowering others, in a world free from strife.

But amidst this change, his heart remains true,
For a man's greatest desire, is to please his woman too.
He understands the power of love's tender embrace,
In her happiness, he finds his own grace.

He listens intently, to the words she imparts,
Her dreams and desires, he holds in his heart.
He supports her ambitions, with unwavering trust,
In her success, he finds his own purpose.

For a man is not complete, without a woman by his side,
Their souls intertwined, on life's joyous ride.
She brings balance and strength, to his very core,
Together they conquer the challenges they explore.

In her presence, he finds solace and peace,
Her love and support never cease.
With her by his side, he can conquer it all,
For in her embrace, he finds his eternal call.

So let us celebrate, the man of today,
A beacon of change, in every possible way.

With respect and understanding, let us stand,
For a man is not complete, without a woman's hand.

IN LOVE'S EMBRACE

In the heart of the man of today, love's tender embrace,
He understands the beauty, the depth, and the grace.
He knows it's not just words, but actions that matter,
To hold and cherish, to make his love shatter.

He knows that love is patient, like the gentle rain,
Nurturing and soothing, erasing all pain.
He listens to her worries, her fears, and her plight,
With empathy and compassion, he holds her tight.

He understands that love is a dance, a rhythmic flow,
Where two souls intertwine, in a delicate show.
He takes her hand and leads, with grace and care,
In every step, he shows how much he's aware.

He knows that love is a shelter, a safe abode,
Where trust and understanding forever unfold.
He provides refuge, in times of storm and strife,
A haven of solace, in the journey of life.

He understands that love is a flame, burning bright,
Igniting their passion, with sparks of delight.
He kindles the fire, with gestures so small,
A touch, a kiss, a whisper that enthralls.

He knows that love is a garden, blooming with care,
Where seeds of affection, they tenderly share.
He nurtures their love, with devotion and time,
Watching it blossoms, in its fragrant prime.

He understands that love is a melody, sweet and pure,
Creating harmonies, that forever endure.

He sings her praises, with words and with song,
A symphony of love, where their hearts belong.

He knows that love is a journey, an endless quest,
Where they explore together, they're very best.
Hand in hand, they traverse life's winding road,
Facing challenges, with love as their code.

So, the man of today, in love's tender embrace,
Understands its essence, with unwavering grace.
He cherishes, he protects, he loves with all his might,
For in love's embrace, he finds his truest light.

WOMAN OF TODAY

In the heart of the woman of today, love's tender embrace,
She understands its power, its beauty, its grace.
She knows it's not just a feeling, but a force so strong,
That carries her through life, where she belongs.

She understands that love is a language, unspoken yet clear,
Expressed through gestures, both small and sincere.
A gentle touch, a warm embrace, a loving gaze,
Conveying her affection in countless ways.

She knows that love is a shelter, a safe harbor,
Where she finds solace, away from the world's clamor.
In his arms, she finds comfort, a place to rest,
A sanctuary of love, where she is forever blessed.

She understands that love is a partnership, a dance,
Where both souls intertwine, taking a chance.
She supports and encourages, through thick and thin,
Building a bond that's unbreakable, from within.

She knows that love is a flame, burning bright,
Igniting their passion, filling every night.
With desire and intimacy, they explore and ignite,
Creating a love that's passionate and right.

She understands that love is a garden, blooming with care,
Where seeds of trust and affection she shares.
Nurturing their love, like a tender flower,
Watching it grows, with each passing hour.

She knows that love is a melody, sweet and pure,
Creating harmonies that will forever endure.

With her words and actions, she sings love's song,
Creating a symphony where hearts belong.

She understands that love is a journey, an adventure,
Where together they navigate and find their center.
Through highs and lows, they face life's trials,
With love as their anchor, their strength never defiles.

So, the woman of today, in love's tender embrace,
Understands its essence, with unwavering grace.
She cherishes, she nurtures, she loves with all her might,
For in love's embrace, she finds her guiding light.

HAND IN HAND

In a world filled with chaos and haste,
There's a couple who's stood the test of time, embraced.
Married for 45 plus years, their love steadfast and true,
On this spontaneous Thursday night, they embark on some-
thing new.

No grand plans or reservations made,
Just a simple night out, like any other escapade.
No fancy attire or extravagant affair,
Just the two of us are a perfect pair.

Hand in hand, they stroll through the town,
Sharing laughter, memories, and stories that abound.
No destination in mind, no agenda to keep,
Just enjoying the moment, as they take a leap.

They find a cozy café, tucked away in a corner street,
Ordering their favorites, savoring the treats.
No need for fancy cuisine or lavish wine,
Just the joy of each other's company, divine.

They reminisce about their early days,
The hurdles they've faced, the love that always stays.
No need for grand gestures or elaborate plans,
Just the comfort of each other's understanding hands.

They walk through the park, under the moon's gentle glow,
Creating new memories, as their love continues to grow.
No need for extravagant gifts or lavish displays,
Just being together, in each other's embrace.

They find a spot to sit under a starlit sky,

Gazing at the constellations, with hearts flying high.
No need for expensive entertainment or extravagant sights,
Just the beauty of nature, igniting their delight.
They dance on the grass, like they did in their youth,
Rekindling the spark, their hearts full of truth.
No need for a crowded dance floor or a fancy ball,
Just the rhythm of their love, entwined in a joyful sprawl.

As the night comes to an end, they hold each other tight,
Grateful for the love that has filled their lives with light.
No need for extravagant gestures or grand displays,
For in the simplicity of this spontaneity everything is light

For they have discovered that true magic lies,
In ordinary moments, where love never dies.
No need for elaborate plans or extravagant affairs,
For their love, after 45 years, is as special as it declares.

ADAPT AND EVOLVE

In the realm of existence, where life abounds,
The truth persists, in every sight and every sound.
Change, the constant companion, forever in our midst,
Life's ever-flowing river, where we cannot resist.

Life is a flux, a dance of endless motion,
A symphony of moments, in perpetual commotion.
Change sweeps through the seasons, like a gentle breeze,
Transforming landscapes, shaking old beliefs.

Change, impartial and neutral, devoid of any guise,
A mirror reflecting truth, where perception lies.
How we perceive it, how we react in kind,
Determines the path we tread, the peace we find.

In the face of change, fear may arise,
As uncertainty looms, casting doubt in our eyes.
But let us not be bound by apprehension's chains,
For change holds the key to growth's fertile plains.

Embrace the ebb and flow, with open arms,
For change, a teacher holds wisdom and charms.
From the ashes of old, new beginnings arise,
Opportunities abound, hidden in disguise.

Amidst the chaos and shifts, find your steady ground,
Adapt and evolve, let resilience be found.
For change may bring challenges, but also chances untold,
To discover hidden strengths, as our stories unfold.

In the tapestry of life, change weaves its thread,
Shaping our journey, where destinies are spread.

Embrace the transformation, let growth be your guide,
For in change's embrace, true liberation resides.

So let us not fear the winds of change's might,
But rather, embrace its whispers in the stillness of the night.
For life's constant flux is a gift we receive,
To shape and mold our path, as we truly believe.

Change is the essence, the rhythm of life's tune,
A reminder that we, too, must adapt and attune.
In the face of change, let us choose our response,
To navigate the unknown with grace and resilience, en-
sconced.

For change is the canvas where our journey unfurls,
A reminder that life is a tapestry of twirls.
Embrace its presence, let go of control,
And dance with change, as it shapes our soul.

INFINITE POWER

In the depths of our being, a realm unseen,
Lies the subconscious, where dreams convene.
A bridge between mind and the infinite source,
Where the five senses gather, a powerful force.

Like a whispering wind, the subconscious breathes,
Guiding our thoughts, like a symphony of leaves.
It holds the key to the mysteries untold,
Connecting us to the universe's fold.

Through sight, it paints a vivid tapestry,
Colors and shapes, a kaleidoscope, we see.
With every glance, a story unfolds,
Infusing our world with stories untold.

Through touch, it weaves a fabric of sensation,
Caressing our skin with delicate elation.
From gentle caresses to the warmth of a hug,
It reminds us of love, like a gentle tug.

Through taste, it savors the flavors of life,
Delighting our palate, removing all strife.
In the sweetness of a berry or the spice of a dish,
It reminds us of joy, a delectable wish.

Through smell, it captures the essence of time,
A fragrance evoking memories sublime.
From the scent of a rose to the smell of the rain,
It transports us to moments we wish to regain.

Through hearing, it listens to the symphony of sound,
The melodic rhythm that surrounds.

From the laughter of a child to the song of the birds,
It fills our world with melodies and words.

The subconscious mind, a gateway profound,
To the infinite power that can be found.
It whispers to us, in subtle ways,
Guiding us through life's mysterious maze.

It holds the wisdom of the ages untold,
A connection to the universe's gold.
Through the five senses, it speaks its truth,
Reminding us of our eternal youth.

So let us listen, with open hearts and minds,
To the whispers of the subconscious, that binds.
For in its depths, lies the infinite power,
Guiding us through life's every hour.

Embrace the subconscious, let it be your guide,
As you navigate the journey, side by side.
For in its embrace, you'll find your way,
To the boundless potential, each and every day.

OUR MEMORIES

In the depths of our minds, memories reside,
A record of moments, where time does confide.
They're the threads that weave our life's grand tapestry,
The lens through which we view the present, future, and
past.

Like whispers from the past, memories arise,
Journeying through time, where nostalgia lies.
They paint vivid pictures of moments gone by,
Imprinting on our souls, like stars in the sky.

Through memories, we relive the joys we've known,
The laughter, the love, the seeds we have sown.
They bring warmth to our hearts on coldest of days,
A beacon of light in life's intricate maze.

But memories can also hold shadows and pain,
The wounds, the losses, the tears like rain.
Yet even in darkness, they offer us strength,
For within our struggles, resilience extends.

Memories shape our present with lessons learned,
A compass guiding us, as bridges are burned.
They remind us of who we once were and can be,
Fueling our growth, setting our spirits free.

With each passing moment, new memories form,
Creating a legacy, weathering life's storm.
They shape the future, like clay in our hands,
As we paint a canvas, where destiny expands.

So cherish each memory, both sweet and bitter,

For they are the essence of who we consider.
They are the lenses through which we perceive,
The past, the present, and what we can achieve.

Let memories guide you with wisdom and grace,
Embrace their whispers as time leaves its trace.
For in their embrace, lies a treasure untold,
A record of life's stories, forever to behold.

MEMORIES AND FUTURE-SELF

Memories, like whispers from a distant shore,
Shape our understanding of the world we explore.
They are the building blocks of our perception,
Weaving together our own unique connection.

Through memories, we learn from days long past,
Lessons etched in our minds, destined to last.
They teach us resilience and strength in adversity,
Transforming challenges into opportunity.

Within the tapestry of memories, we hold dear,
Our identity takes form, becoming crystal clear.
They reflect our triumphs, our struggles, our joys,
Crafting a narrative that no one can destroy.

Memories construct the bridge to our future,
Guiding our steps, like a steadfast tutor.
They help us envision the person we aspire to be,
Creating a roadmap to the future we see.

With each memory, we paint a vibrant scene,
Imagining the person we're destined to glean.
They inspire our actions, our dreams, and desires,
Igniting the spark that fuels our inner fires.

But memories alone cannot shape our fate,
They are seeds, but we must cultivate.
Through choices and actions, we mold our own way,
Crafting a future self, day by day.

So let memories be our compass, our guide,
Nurturing growth, with each step we stride.

They hold the power to shape our destiny,
As we navigate life's vast, mysterious sea.

A GLIMPSE OF PROGRESS

In the tapestry of time, a week so profound,
Let me reflect on the progress I have found.
Moments that shimmered with growth and delight,
In this poetic ode, I'll paint them in light.

A deep and meaningful it flowed,
With wisdom and insight, it surely bestowed.
Ideas exchanged, perspectives intertwined,
A glimpse of progress in the seeds of my mind.

An event that challenged, pushed me to the brink,
Yet I stood tall, refusing to shrink.
Through obstacles faced, I found strength untold,
A testament to progress, a story to unfold.

Experiences that stretched me, made me explore,
Unveiling new talents, I never knew before.
In each endeavor, a step forward I made,
Progress etched in every choice I've weighed.

A small victory, perhaps, but immense in its worth,
A goal accomplished, a dream brought forth.
The satisfaction that comes from tasks complete,
A reminder that progress is ever so sweet.

And in the quiet moments, when I looked within,
I saw the growth that resides deep within.
A sense of self-awareness, a clearer sight,
Progress manifested in my inner light.

So let this poem serve as a testament true,
To the progress made in this past week's view.

Events, conversations, experiences so grand,
A reflection of the progress I now understand.
For progress is not always quantified by leaps,
But in the small steps, the progress seeps.
And as I journey on, with each passing day,
I'll celebrate the progress that comes my way.

BEHOLD A BEAUTIFUL SUNRISE

As the darkness fades into the horizon's embrace,
A new dawn emerges with gentle grace.
The sky ablaze with hues so divine,
A symphony of colors, a celestial sign.

Behold the beauty of the sunrise's glow,
A tapestry of gold, a vibrant show.
The world awakens, bathed in golden light,
A promise of a new day, shining bright.

With each sunrise, a new beginning is born,
A chance to embrace life, to be reborn.
The day unfolds like a precious gift,
Filled with endless possibilities, our spirits lift.

In the gentle rays of the morning sun,
We find solace, a moment of peace won.
The world stirs, as nature comes alive,
Whispering secrets, as we strive to thrive.

Each dawn brings hope, a renewed desire,
To chase our dreams, to reach higher.
With each new day, a blank canvas we see,
An opportunity to create, to be set free.

The sunrise reminds us of life's precious worth,
A reminder to cherish every moment of birth.
To dance with joy, to savor every taste,
To embrace the beauty, not let it go to waste.

So let us greet each sunrise with open hearts,
Embrace the unknown, as each new day starts.

For in this promise, we find endless grace,
A chance to experience life's vibrant embrace.

With each new sunrise, the world is renewed,
A symphony of hope, a melody imbued.
So let us embrace the gift each day brings,
And soar on the wings of dawn's gentle wings.

EMOTIONS DIVINE

With each sunrise, emotions come alive,
A kaleidoscope of feelings, ready to thrive.
The dawn's first light ignites a flame within,
An array of emotions, a journey to begin.

Hope rises like the sun, casting away despair,
Promising a fresh start, a chance to repair.
It whispers softly, "Today is a new day,
With endless possibilities, don't let them slip away."

Excitement dances in the golden rays,
Anticipation of adventures that lie in wait.
A sense of wonder fills the waking air,
As dreams take flight, hopes beyond compare.

Peace settles gently in the morning glow,
Calmness enveloping, like a tranquil flow.
The chaos of the world momentarily stills,
In the embrace of the sunrise, all worries are distilled.

Gratitude blossoms like flowers at dawn,
Thankfulness for the blessings to be drawn.
For the gift of life, for the beauty that surrounds,
The sunrise's splendor, in awe we are bound.

Reflection lingers in the early light,
As the world awakens, a moment to unite.
Thoughts wander, memories start to unfurl,
Emotions intertwined, like a precious pearl.

Inspiration sparks with the rising sun,
Creativity ignited, a new chapter begun.

The colors of the sky, the melodies in the air,
Stir the depths of the soul, igniting passions rare.

And in the heart, a bittersweet embrace,
For with each sunrise, time continues its chase.
Emotions intertwine, a delicate dance,
As the morning sun illuminates life's expanse.

So let the emotions of each sunrise unfurl,
A symphony of feelings, a vibrant whirl.
From hope to gratitude, from peace to inspiration,
Each sunrise brings forth an emotional transformation.

Embrace the emotions that the sunrise brings,
Let them guide you as you spread your wings.
For with each new day, a canvas to create,
And the sunrise's emotions, your soul shall elate.

A COSMIC DANCE

In the realm of the minuscule, where atoms reside,
A dance of cosmic proportions takes place inside.
These building blocks of matter, so tiny and dense,
Hold secrets untold, a mysterious essence.

Atoms, the fundamental units of creation,
Unite and bond, forming molecules in elation.
Through valence and electrons, they connect and entwine,
Creating a symphony of structures divine.

But behold, in the vast expanse of space,
Atoms and molecules find their own special place.
They shift and rearrange, assuming new form,
A metamorphosis, a molecular storm.

In this waltz of configurations, ever evolving,
Particles within transform with resolve unswerving.
Behaviors shift, like a cosmic ballet,
The essence of matter takes a different display.

Through energy and forces, this transformation occurs,
Electromagnetic interactions, nature's subtle concurs.
Atoms and molecules, in their dynamic embrace,
Create diversity, a universe of grace.

So, marvel at the dance of atoms and molecules,
Their ability to shape-shift, to constantly amuse.
From solid to liquid, gas, and even more,
Their ever-changing nature, we cannot ignore.

In the grand tapestry of existence, we find,
Atoms and molecules, a captivating bind.

Their configurations in space, a cosmic play,
Where the behavior of particles takes sway.

ATOMS AND MOLECULES

In the realm of creation, where wonders abound,
Atoms and molecules, building blocks are found.
These tiny entities, so full of potential,
Hold the power to shape and transform, so essential.

Within their core, atoms hold their secrets tight,
Nucleus and electrons, a captivating sight.
Through bonds and forces, they come together,
Creating molecules, a spectacle to treasure.

But what causes this transformation, you may ask,
What catalysts guide this intricate task?
It is the dance of energy, both fierce and serene,
That propels atoms and molecules to intervene.

Temperature and pressure, like invisible hands,
Can alter their configurations, as nature commands.
A rise in heat, a change in environment's embrace,
Atoms and molecules respond in a graceful chase.

Chemical reactions, a symphony of change,
Atoms rearrange, their structure rearranged.
Electrons shift, bonds break and form anew
A transformational journey, forever true.

Within the realm of creation, atoms an
They are the architects of nature's di
From solid to liquid, gas, and even
Their configurations in flux, an

Atoms and molecules, consi
The essence of matter, the

They form the foundation, the fabric of existence,
Their transformations, a testament of persistence.

So, marvel at these wonders, so small and yet grand,
Atoms and molecules, the artists of this land.
In their configurations, a symphony we trace,
Guided by the forces that shape our cosmic space.

TRANSFORMATION IS CONSTANT

The building blocks of creation, at the core,
Are atoms, the fundamental units we explore.
These minuscule particles, so diverse and vast,
Combine and interact to form a lasting cast.

Atoms themselves consist of a nucleus within,
Protons and neutrons, tightly bound therein.
Electrons orbit, in energy levels they reside,
Creating a balance, a dance of forces they abide.

When atoms come together, in a cosmic ballet,
Molecules are born, in a captivating display.
Through chemical bonding, they unite and combine,
Sharing electrons, their configurations align.

Covalent bonds form when atoms share,
Electrons between them, creating a pair.
Ionic bonds, on the other hand, arise,
When electrons are transferred, attracting nearby.

Factors that cause transformation, indeed,
Are plentiful, each with its unique creed.
Temperature, for one, can induce a change,
Increasing energy, making atoms rearrange.

Pressure also plays a significant role,
Squeezing atoms tightly, influencing their whole.
Catalysts, too, can spark a transformation,
Speeding up reactions, with their activation.

Light and radiation, with their energetic might,
Can excite atoms, altering their state in sight.

Electric and magnetic fields, they wield,
Manipulating atoms, their configurations yield.
In the realm of creation, these factors combine,
Causing atoms and molecules to realign.
Through a symphony of forces and energy's sway,
Transformations occur, shaping our world every day.

LIKE GRAINS OF SAND

In the realm of creation, a tapestry we weave,
A symphony of life, where moments interleave.
From the blocks of existence, we're formed and shaped,
Human beings, evolving, in this world we're draped.

Every day, we rise with the dawn's gentle kiss,
Transforming with purpose, in moments of bliss.
Like atoms and molecules, we bond and connect,
Creating relationships, love and respect.

In the minutes that pass, our potential unfurls,
As we navigate challenges and dreams, we unfurl.
We learn and we grow as time slips away,
Transforming our thoughts, with each passing day.

In the hours that follow, we toil and we strive,
Building our lives, keeping dreams alive.
With passion and dedication, we shape our path,
Transforming our future, avoiding the aftermath.
And as seconds tick by, like grains of sand,
We make choices, both big and unplanned.
Transformations occur, in moments so brief,
Shaping our character, beyond belief.

Through joy and through sorrow, we find our own way,
Transforming our perspectives, embracing each day.
With resilience and hope, we face every test,
Creating a life that we deem to be best.

So let us remember, as we journey on,
That transformation is constant, from dusk until dawn.

We are the architects of our own creation,
Transforming our world with determination.

In the blocks of creation, we find our true worth,
As human beings, transforming the Earth.
May we embrace the power within our core,
And create a world, where love and peace endure.

TIME LEAVES ITS TRACE
(OR TIME SLIPS AWAY)

As time slips away, a subtle dance unfolds,
Moments become memories, stories yet untold.
The present becomes past, slipping through our grasp,
Leaving traces of moments, fading in a gasp.

The young turn old, as days swiftly pass by,
Lines etched on faces, like a painted sky.
Youthful vigor fades, as wisdom takes its place,
Leaving behind a legacy, leaving a trace.

Relationships evolve, as time slips away,
Some grow stronger, while others may fray.
Friendships forged in fire, tested by the years,
Bonds that withstand, even through the tears.

Dreams once held close, may fade or transform,
New aspirations emerge, like a brewing storm.
Opportunities arise, and paths may diverge,
As time's gentle nudge pushes us to surge.

The world spins on, as time slips away,
Seasons change, and nights turn into day.
We witness history unfold, in each passing hour,
Leaving imprints on hearts, like a blooming flower.

But amidst the fleeting, there's beauty to be found,
In the precious present, where life's joys abound.
Cherishing every second, every breath we take,
Embracing the moments, for our own sake.

So, as time slips away, let's seize the day,
Carving memories, along with life's winding way.
For in the tapestry of life, each moment has its place,
A reminder to cherish, as time leaves its trace.

THE BEAUTY OF TIME

In the realm of time, where moments swiftly fly,
We search for ways to pause, to still the sky.
But time, relentless, refuses to be tamed,
Its ceaseless march, forever unashamed.

Yet in the fleeting nature of each passing hour,
There lies a beauty, a hidden source of power.
For time's fluidity, its ever-changing face,
Allows us to find beauty in its transient grace.

In the rising sun, painting colors on the dawn,
Or in the dew-kissed petals, on a flower's lawn.
The fleeting moments, like whispers in the breeze,
Hold a beauty that's found in how swiftly they seize.

The laughter shared with loved ones, in joyful delight,
Or the tears shed in sorrow, on a melancholy night.
These emotions, fleeting as they may be,
Teach us the depth of our humanity.

In the dance of seasons, in nature's grand display,
We witness the passage of time, in its own unique way.
From the blossoming of spring to the fall's golden hue,
Each fleeting moment offers a different view.

For time, though elusive, carries gifts untold,
Lessons of growth, of resilience, and of being bold.
It teaches us to savor, to hold close and let go,
To find beauty in the transient, as life continues to flow.

So, while we cannot stop time's relentless stride,
We can embrace its fleeting nature, with arms open wide.

Finding beauty in each passing moment's grace,
Knowing that in impermanence, life finds its trace.

For in the ebb and flow of time's eternal stream,
We learn to cherish, to appreciate, to dream.
And in the beauty of the transient, we find our way,
Embracing life's fleeting moments, come what may.

EMBRACING LIFE'S JOURNEY

In the tapestry of life, where time unfolds,
Lessons abound, as each moment molds.
For time, a teacher, with wisdom to impart,
Whispers in our ears, a gentle call to start.

In the racing seconds, the minutes that flee,
Time reminds us of life's brevity.
A precious gift, bestowed upon our birth,
To cherish and embrace, for all it's worth.

With every tick, a reminder to be present,
To live fully, with hearts luminescent.
For in the passing seconds, we find the key,
To unlock the beauty of our destiny.

Time teaches us to savor, to seize the day,
To dance in the rain, to laugh, to play.
To relish the flavors, the joys that abound,
And create memories that forever resound.

In the face of adversity, time lends its hand,
Guiding us through darkness, helping us stand.
With each challenge, a chance to grow and learn,
To rise above, and with resilience, return.

In the embrace of loved ones, time whispers love,
Reminding us to cherish, to hold close, and to shove.
The limitations that keep our hearts apart,
For time teaches us that love is a work of art.

Through seasons of change, time paints a scene,
From vibrant spring to winter's serene.

It shows us the cycles, the beauty in transition,
And how growth emerges from life's intermission.

So let us not be idle, as time slips away,
But rather, embrace it, in every possible way.
For every minute, every second we're given,
Is a chance to live fully, to be truly driven.

Let's seize the fleeting moments, with boundless delight,
And fill our lives with purpose, with passion, and light.
For time, our teacher imparts a truth so clear,
To embrace and enjoy ourselves while we're here.

So as the hands of the clock continue to move,
Let us dance to the rhythm, find our own groove.
Embracing life's journey, in all its grandeur,
For time lessons teach us, to live, to remember.

IN THE FACE OF CHALLENGE

In the depths of adversity, when shadows loom,
Time emerges as a guiding light, dispelling gloom.
With each passing moment, it whispers a tale,
Of strength and resilience, that will never fail.

When hardships befall, and the road seems rough,
Time reminds us that nothing is ever enough.
For it carries us forward, through trials and strife,
Guiding us towards the essence of a meaningful life.

In the face of challenges, time becomes our guide,
Leading us through darkness, where hope may hide.
With every step we take, it offers a hand,
Showing us the way, helping us understand.

Time teaches us patience, in the midst of despair,
That healing and growth need moments to repair.
Through the depths of sorrow, it shows us the way,
To embrace resilience and find strength each day.

In the tapestry of life, time weaves a thread,
A reminder that storms, too, shall tread.
For it knows that adversities shape and define,
The strength within us, that will always shine.

With the passage of time, wounds start to heal,
Scars become stories, our resilience revealed.
Time offers perspective, a broader view,
Adversity's lessons can make us anew.

In the crucible of trials, time molds our soul,
Nurturing resilience, making us whole.

It teaches us to rise when we fall and stumble,
To find the strength within and not crumble.

So, when adversity knocks, and challenges arise,
Let time be our compass, our guiding prize.
For it holds the wisdom, the lessons we need,
To navigate through adversity and succeed.

With time as our mentor, we'll endure and grow,
Through every storm, we'll find a way to glow.
For time, the guardian will never let us stray,
Guiding us through adversity, each step of the way.

THE ELIXIR OF LIFE

In the realm of nature, where life begins,
Water flows, a miracle that never dims.
Its gentle touch, a soothing embrace,
A symphony of coherence, filling every space.

Water, the elixir of life, pure and clear,
Quenching our thirst, removing our fear.
It nourishes our bodies, keeps us alive,
A precious resource, on which we thrive.

From the mighty oceans to the tranquil streams,
Water sustains us, fulfilling our dreams.
It cleanses our being, purifies our soul,
A source of vitality, making us whole.

In the morning dew, a shimmering display,
Water brings life to flowers, in a magical way.
Coherence in action, as petals unfold,
Beauty in harmony, a story untold.

Consider the rivers, flowing with grace,
Coherently carving landscapes, leaving a trace.
They shape the earth, with unwavering force,
A testament to water's incredible course.

For human beings, water is a gift,
A necessity for survival, our spirits uplift.
It quenches our thirst, hydrates our cells,
And in its coherence, our wellness excels.

Imagine a hot summer's day, sun blazing high,
A sip of cool water, relief drawing nigh.

Or a refreshing swim, in a crystal-clear lake,
Revitalizing our bodies, for goodness' sake.

Water's coherence extends beyond our thirst,
It's essential for health, as we've come to trust.
It aids digestion, regulates body temperature,
A vital element, for every creature.

Consider the healing power it holds,
In therapies, its magic unfolds.
From hydrotherapy to calming baths,
Water's coherence eases life's aftermaths.

So, cherish water, this gift from above,
A symbol of life, a source of love.
Its coherence brings harmony to our core,
Nurturing our well-being, forevermore.

COHERENCE WATER

In the realm of wellness, where healing resides,
Coherence water flows, a balm that provides,
Its gentle touch, a soothing embrace,
Healing energy, filling every space.

Coherence water, a symphony of grace,
Restoring balance, at a steady pace.
Its harmonious vibrations, a healing song,
Revitalizing body, mind, and soul, strong.

Imagine a weary soul seeking solace,
Coherence water, a remedy to embrace.
In its presence, stress begins to fade,
A tranquil oasis, where calm is made.

For those burdened with pain, aching and sore,
Coherence water offers relief, and more.
Its healing properties, like a gentle tide,
Easing discomfort, bringing healing inside.

Consider the athlete, pushing their limits,
Coherence water, a source that replenishes.
Hydrating their body, enhancing their flow,
Optimizing performance, helping them grow.

In the realm of emotions, where turmoil may dwell,
Coherence water brings peace, we can tell.
Its coherent vibrations calming the mind,
Restoring clarity, leaving worries behind.

For those seeking clarity, a path to explore,
Coherence water, a guide to restore.

It aligns the thoughts, clears away the fog,
Unlocking wisdom, like a gentle jog.

Imagine a troubled heart, burdened with grief,
Coherence water, a source of relief.
Its coherent frequencies, soothing the pain,
Healing the wounds, like a gentle rain.

For those on a journey of spiritual growth,
Coherence water, a catalyst for both.
It amplifies intentions, creating a space,
For manifesting dreams, with divine grace.

Consider the power it holds in its flow,
Coherence water, a healer we know.
From ancient traditions to modern-day,
Its benefits, profound, paving the way.

So, embrace coherence water, let it be,
A source of healing, for you and me.
Its gentle touch, a remedy so grand,
Bringing harmony, with a loving hand.

A PRECIOUS RESOURCE

In the realm of nature, where life begins,
Water flows, a miracle that never dims.
Its gentle touch, a soothing embrace,
A symphony of coherence, filling every space.

Water, the elixir of life, pure and clear,
Quenching our thirst, removing our fear.
It nourishes our bodies, keeps us alive,
A precious resource, on which we thrive.

From the mighty oceans to the tranquil streams,
Water sustains us, fulfilling our dreams.
It cleanses our being, purifies our soul,
A source of vitality, making us whole.

In the morning dew, a shimmering display,
Water brings life to flowers, in a magical way.
Coherence in action, as petals unfold,
Beauty in harmony, a story untold.

Consider the rivers, flowing with grace,
Coherently carving landscapes, leaving a trace.
They shape the earth, with unwavering force,
A testament to water's incredible course.

For human beings, water is a gift,
A necessity for survival, our spirits uplift.
It quenches our thirst, hydrates our cells,
And in its coherence, our wellness excels.

Imagine a hot summer's day, sun blazing high,
A sip of cool water, relief drawing nigh.

Or a refreshing swim, in a crystal-clear lake,
Revitalizing our bodies, for goodness' sake.

Water's coherence extends beyond our thirst,
It's essential for health, as we've come to trust.
It aids digestion, regulates body temperature,
A vital element, for every creature.

Consider the healing power it holds,
In therapies, magic unfolds.
From hydrotherapy to calming baths,
Water's coherence eases life's aftermaths.

So, cherish water, this gift from above,
A symbol of life, a source of love.
Its coherence brings harmony to our core,
Nurturing our well-being, forevermore.

A BRILLIANT MIND

Ralph Waldo Emerson, a brilliant mind,
Contemplated the role of poetry, he did find.
He believed it held great importance, you see,
In educating and inspiring humanity.

For Emerson, poetry was a sacred art,
A means to touch the depths of the heart.
Through its words, he sought to unveil,
The truths and wisdom that could never fail.

Poetry, to him, was a source of light,
Guiding souls through darkness, day or night.
It had the power to awaken dormant minds,
And bridge the gaps that society often finds.

In his essay, "The Poet," Emerson explained,
That poets were the true seers, unchained.
They could see beyond the surface of things,
And capture the beauty that life often brings.

He believed that poets had a divine gift,
To uplift and inspire, their words could lift.
By expressing emotions and thoughts profound,
They could spark change and turn the world around.

Emerson cited examples of poets of old,
Those words still resonate, powerful and bold.
From Homer's epics to Shakespeare's sonnets,
Their poetry transcends time, never forgotten.

Through the verses of Whitman, he saw,
The celebration of democracy, without flaw.

And in the works of Wordsworth and Keats,
He found solace and beauty, a joy that repeats.

So, let us embrace poetry's profound worth,
For it holds the power to transform and unearth.
The truths and passions that lie within,
And inspire us to live a life that's akin.

For in Emerson's eyes, poetry had a role,
To educate and inspire, to make us whole.
So let us cherish this art form divine,
And let its words forever in our hearts shine.

CATALYST OF THOUGHT

In the eyes of Emerson, poets held great might,
Their words had the power to ignite,
A flame of change in society's heart,
And through their verses, a new world could start.

The power of poets, he firmly believed,
Was in their ability to perceive,
The truths hidden beneath the surface, unseen,
And share them with the world, pure and keen.

They were the seers, the visionaries of their time,
Capturing emotions, thoughts sublime,
Their words had the strength to move and inspire,
To set hearts ablaze with a burning desire.

Through their verses, poets could expose,
The injustices that society chose,
To turn a blind eye to, to pretend not to see,
But poets, they saw and spoke fearlessly.

They brought light to the darkness, hope to despair,
Challenging the status quo, daring to care,
Their words were a balm for the wounded soul,
A catalyst for change, making society whole.

Emerson saw poets as the catalysts of thought,
Guiding humanity to the wisdom they sought,
Through their poems, they could shape and mold,
A better world, where love and truth would unfold.

Emerson praised Whitman's bold verse,
That celebrated democracy, breaking the curse,

Of division and inequality, embracing all,
His words united, breaking down every wall.

And Wordsworth, with his nature-inspired rhymes,
Awakened in people a love for simpler times,
His poems connected them to the beauty of the earth,
Urging them to protect it, to understand its worth.

Poets hold a vital role in society's quest,
To create a world that's fair and blessed,
Their words have the power to heal and transform,
To inspire positive change, in every form.

In Emerson's view, poets were the guiding light,
Leading us towards what is just and right,
Their words, like seeds, planted in fertile ground,
Could grow a garden of hope, profound.

So let us cherish the power of poets, we must,
For they hold within them the power to adjust,
The course of society, to shape its destiny,
And lead us towards a better future of mankind.

THE POWER TO UPLIFT

Emerson's praise for poets, oh so grand,
Their words like music, a symphony in hand,
He lauded their vision, their power to see,
The depths of truth, the wonders that be.

Whitman, the bard of democracy's call,
His verses embraced one and all,
In "Leaves of Grass," he celebrated the free,
Breaking down barriers, for all to see.
Emerson saw in Whitman the spirit of unity,
His words are a beacon of hope, a bridge to community,
Through his poems, he championed equality's fight,
And urged us to embrace diversity with delight.
Wordsworth, the poet of nature's embrace,
His verses took us to tranquil and sacred space,
He saw in nature a source of solace and grace,
A teacher of lessons, a sanctuary's embrace.

Emerson admired Wordsworth's connection so deep,
His poetic lens, a window to secrets to keep,
Through his odes to nature, he urged us to see,
The beauty and truth that reside in every tree.

Emerson himself, a poet revered,
His words are like wisdom, always endeared,
He preached self-reliance, and the power within,
To trust our own instincts, to let our true selves begin.

His essays and poems, a beacon of light,
Guiding us through darkness, with insight,

Emerson's praise for poets was not in vain,
For their words have the power to heal and sustain.

So let us remember the poets Emerson admired,
Their words, like fire, forever inspired,
They showed us the path to a brighter tomorrow,
Through their verses, we banished sorrow.

For poets, they hold a sacred role,
To uplift spirits, to touch the soul,
Their words, like wings, can set us free,
And guide us towards the best we can be.

So, let us cherish the poets who ignite,
The flames of change, with their words so bright,
Emerson's praise, a testament to their might,
For poets, they bring us joy and insight.

THE POWER OF LOVE

In the realm of love, a tapestry divine,
Where hearts entwine, and emotions align,
Let me share a poem, a gentle decree,
On how to show love, for our loved ones to see.

Love is a language, spoken not in words,
But in actions, gestures, and kindness heard.
To make them realize, deep in their core,
That they are cherished, forevermore.

To show love, we must listen with care,
To their hopes, dreams, and burdens they bear.
To lend a hand, and offer our support,
In their triumphs and trials, always exhort.

Love is an embrace, a gentle touch,
A comforting presence, when times get rough.
To hold them close, and wipe away tears,
Showing them love, erasing their fears.

Love is a gift, that knows no bounds,
In the simplest acts, it can be found.
A kind word, a smile, a warm embrace,
Can light up their world, leave a lasting trace.

Love is patient, a beacon of grace,
Accepting flaws and giving space.
To love unconditionally, without demand,
To be their rock, forever on hand.

So, dear friend, know that you are loved,
By God above, and those you hold beloved.

Like Jesus on the cross, His love so vast,
Rest assured, that God's love will forever last.

For love is a language that needs no voice,
It speaks through actions, the ultimate choice.
To show love to others, and let them see,
That they are loved and will eternally be.

DIVINE LOVE

In depths of time, a love was born,
A love that's boundless, forever sworn.
From the heavens above, it cascades down,
God's love, a treasure, that knows no frown.

Unfathomable, this love divine,
In every heart, it seeks to shine.
A love that's steadfast, unwavering and true,
Embracing us all, no matter what we do.

In the darkest nights, when shadows loom,
God's love is there, a guiding light in the gloom.
A beacon of hope, a comforting embrace,
Filling our souls with eternal grace.

With gentle whispers, God's love is heard,
In the rustling leaves, in each singing bird.
In the laughter of children, in the gentle breeze,
God's love surrounds us, puts our hearts at ease.

It is a love that forgives, without condition,
Washing away our sins, with divine remission.
A love that heals wounds, both seen and unseen,
Rebuilding broken hearts, making them pristine.

God's love is patient, enduring and kind,
In every moment, it's there to find.
It knows no boundaries, no limits or bounds,
Reaching out to all, with love that resounds.

In the beauty of nature, God's love is displayed,
In every sunrise and sunset, its glory portrayed.

In the vastness of the universe, so grand,
God's love is present, holding us in His hand.

So let us embrace this love, so pure,
Let it guide our steps and help us endure.
For in God's love, we find solace and peace,
A love that will never fade but only increase.

In every breath we take, in every beat of our heart,
God's love is there, a masterpiece of art.
So let us bask in this love divine,
And share it with others, for all of time.

For God's love is infinite, it knows no end,
A love that's unbreakable, a love to transcend.
So let us celebrate this love, forevermore,
In awe of God's love, our spirits shall soar.

SHE STANDS FOR ALL WOMEN

In the strength of a woman, a power untold,
Lies a truth that resonates, a story to unfold.
With each step she takes with courage and grace,
She stands for all women, in every time and place.

In the face of adversity, she finds her voice,
A warrior of justice, her spirit will rejoice.
For when she stands up, in her own unique way,
She paves the path for others, lighting the way.

Her strength is not selfish, it's a collective might,
A beacon of hope, shining through the night.
For in her triumphs and struggles, she carries a flame,
Igniting the fire of change, in each woman's name.

She may not realize the impact she holds,
With every word spoken, with stories untold.
But in her defiance, in her unwavering stance,
She becomes the embodiment of a powerful dance.

Through her battles fought, she breaks the mold,
Unleashing the power that lies untold.
For in her liberation, she sets others free,
Inspiring a movement, for all women to see.

With every hurdle crossed, with every barrier shattered,
She stands for all women, their dreams and what mattered.
For her strength is contagious, a force to be reckoned,
A reminder to all, that their voices too can beckon.

So let us celebrate the women, who stand tall,
For they are the pillars, the voices that call.

May their courage inspire, may their stories be heard,
As they pave the way for a more equal world.

For each time a woman stands up, without knowing,
She stands for all women, her power showing.
In unity, in sisterhood, we rise hand in hand,
For when one woman stands, we all understand.

GRIT AND DETERMINATION

Success is not solely found in greatness's glare,
But in the steady steps taken, with utmost care.
It's not a fleeting moment, a mere stroke of luck,
But the result of consistency, hard work unstuck.

For greatness, it may come, but it's not the sole aim,
It's the byproduct of effort, the fruit of the game.
It's the culmination of hours, days, and years,
Of dedication and perseverance, despite the fears.

Success is a journey, a path that we tread,
With every step forward, a lesson to be spread.
It's not about shortcuts, or instant acclaim,
But the commitment to excellence, the relentless aim.

The road may be long, with obstacles galore,
But with grit and determination, we'll endure.
Through setbacks and failures, we'll rise again,
For success is not about how, but when.

Consistency is key, a steadfast resolve,
To keep pushing forward, to constantly evolve.
It's the small steps taken, day after day,
That leads to achievements, paving the way.

Hard work is the foundation, the solid ground,
That supports the dreams, where success is found.
It's the sweat and the tears, the sacrifices made,
That sculpt our destiny, where greatness is laid.

And as we toil and strive, with unwavering dedication,
Success will find us, without hesitation.

For greatness is not the destination, but a part of the race,
And with consistency and hard work, we'll find our place.

So let us embrace the journey, with open hearts,
Knowing that success is not about playing the parts.
It's about the effort we put forth, day by day,
And greatness will follow, in its own special way.

POWER IS ON YOUR HANDS

In the realm of thoughts, where our minds wander free,
Lies a truth to ponder, a notion for you and me.
For if we don't choose the thoughts we let inside,
Others may shape our perceptions, where motives may hide.

In this vast sea of ideas, opinions, and views,
We must be mindful of what we choose to peruse.
For every thought and image, like a seed it may sow,
Influencing our beliefs, the direction we go.

If we let others dictate the thoughts we consume,
Their motives may not be pure, their intentions in bloom.
They may seek to manipulate, to control our minds,
Leaving us vulnerable, with thoughts that are confined.

But fear not, for we hold the power within,
To choose the thoughts and images that align.
To seek knowledge and wisdom, with discerning eyes,
And let our own motives be the highest prize.

Let us be guardians of our mental domain,
Filtering out negativity, embracing the humane.
Let love and compassion guide our thoughts each day,
And keep the darkness at bay, in every possible way.

For when we choose our thoughts with care and grace,
We create a sanctuary, a sacred inner space.
A place where truth and goodness can freely reside,
And our own motives shine, as a beacon of pride.

Remember, dear friend, the power is in your hands,

To shape your thoughts, like an artist's masterful plans.
Choose wisely the thoughts and images you embrace,
And let your own motives be the highest, with unwavering grace.

POWER TO SHAPE OUR WORLD

In the realm of thoughts, where dreams are born,
We hold the power to shape the world adorned.
With careful selection, thoughts become art,
Creating a masterpiece, a work of the heart.

With care and grace, we choose each thought,
Like a sculptor crafting, emotions sought.
With every choice, brushstroke applied,
A canvas of life, where dreams coincide.

Thoughts of love, like petals in bloom,
Create a garden, dispelling all gloom.
Kindness and compassion, seeds we sow,
Nurturing connections, watching them grow.

With thoughts of courage, we conquer fear,
Breaking down barriers, drawing near.
Limitations shattered, boundaries no more,
Creating a path to dreams we adore.

Thoughts of gratitude, like shimmering light,
Illuminate the darkest night.
Appreciating life's blessings, big and small,
Creating a tapestry, woven with awe.

With thoughts of hope, we build a bridge,
Overcoming obstacles, inch by inch.
Believing in possibilities, untold,
Creating a future, shining like gold.

Thoughts of creativity, a boundless well,
Unleash imagination, stories to tell.

Painting with words, melodies in the air,
Creating beauty, beyond compare.

So let us choose our thoughts with care,
For they hold the power to build or impair.
With grace and intention, let's create,
A world where love and harmony resonate.

For in the realm of thoughts, our minds unfold,
And what we create, forever behold.
With care and grace, let our thoughts be true,
And watch as our dreams become life's breakthrough.

WINGS TO OUR SOUL

When obstacles loom and darkness surrounds,
Thoughts of hope emerge, like whispers of sound.
They carry us forward, on wings of belief,
Guiding us through challenges, offering relief.

In the face of adversity, when all seems lost,
Thoughts of hope ignite, no matter the cost.
They fuel our determination, steady our stride,
And with unwavering faith, we conquer the tide.

Like a beacon of light on a stormy night,
Thoughts of hope illuminate our path, shining bright.
They remind us of possibilities, yet unseen,
And inspire us to pursue what we deem.

When doubts cloud our minds, and fears take hold,
Thoughts of hope remind us we're strong and bold.
They whisper encouragement, a gentle embrace,
Emboldening us to rise and keep up the pace.

As we navigate the twists and turns of life's maze,
Thoughts of hope infuse us with unwavering gaze.
They remind us that setbacks are mere steppingstones,
Leading us closer to the dreams we've known.

In times of despair, when all seems bleak,
Thoughts of hope provide the solace we seek.
They remind us that within us lies a fire,
To overcome challenges and rise even higher.

Like a seedling breaking through the frozen ground,
Thoughts of hope push us forward, unbound.

They remind us of the strength we possess,
To overcome obstacles and achieve success.

So let thoughts of hope fill your heart and mind,
In the face of adversity, they'll help you find,
The courage to persevere, to keep pushing through,
And overcome obstacles, old and new.

For thoughts of hope are like wings to our soul,
They lift us up, helping us reach our goal.
With hope as our guide, we'll rise above,
And conquer each challenge with strength and love.

BEND REALITY TO YOUR WILL

In the realm where thoughts collide,
Where dreams and reality coincide,
There lies a power, hidden deep within,
A force that defies what we've always been.

Think about it, get it, the mantra resounds,
Harness the power, let your desires astound.
For in the science of human vibration,
Lies are the key to shaping our own creation.

Like a tuning fork, our thoughts hold sway,
Sending ripples into the universe's array.
Energy flows, in frequencies we send,
And what we focus on, we ultimately transcend.

Belief is the catalyst, the spark that ignites,
Unleashing the power, setting things right.
When we align our thoughts with intention,
We unlock the door to manifest our vision.

Visualize the life you wish to embrace,
With clarity and focus, in every space.
See it, feel it, let it become real,
As your thoughts and reality begin to congeal.

But beware, for doubt can cast a shadow,
Blocking the flow, impeding the glow.
Stay true to your vision, unwavering in trust,
And watch as reality bends to adjust.

Thoughts of abundance, thoughts of love,
Thoughts of gratitude, soaring above.

Harness the power, let your mind soar,
And watch as miracles unfold, like never before.

For the universe listens, responds to our call,
Aligning the stars, breaking down every wall.
Think about it, get it, let the vibrations align,
And watch as your reality begins to intertwine.

So tap into the science of human vibration,
Embrace the power, with unwavering dedication.
Think about it, get it, let your dreams take flight,
As you bend reality to your will, with all your might.

CREATING YOUR OWN REALITY

In the realm where intention meets the mind,
A powerful dance begins to unwind.
For when we align our thoughts just right,
A wondrous transformation takes flight.

With focused intention, our dreams take hold,
The universe listens; its secrets unfold.
Every thought, every desire we send,
Becomes a force that knows no end.

As we align our thoughts with pure intent,
As the energy shifts, the path becomes bent.
Obstacles crumble, pathways appear,
With every step, our vision grows clear.

Aligned with purpose, our hearts ignite,
A flame of passion, burning bright.
The universe conspires, aligning the stars,
Guiding us forward, removing all bars.

In this state of alignment, we find our power,
A beacon of light in the darkest hour.
Our thoughts and actions in perfect sync,
Manifesting miracles, in a single blink.

With intention as our guiding force,
We chart a course, uncharted, off course.
The possibilities endless, the sky the limit,
As we align our thoughts, we truly commit.

The law of attraction, in full display,
Bringing forth blessings, day by day.

We magnetize abundance, love, and joy,
As our intentions manifest, we become the envoy.

Align your thoughts with unwavering belief,
Let go of doubt, embrace the relief.
For when intention and thoughts align,
A world of possibilities, we shall find.

In this dance of alignment, we discover our might,
Creating a reality that shines so bright.
So let your intentions guide your way,
And watch as magic unfolds, day by day.

THE UNIVERSE LISTENS

In the vast expanse of the cosmic sea,
Our focused intentions hold the key.
For the Universe listens, it hears our call,
Responding with grace, to one and all.

When our minds align, with purpose and might,
The Universe senses our beacon of light.
It gathers our desires, like whispers on the wind,
And begins to orchestrate, the magic within.

With focused intentions, our thoughts take flight,
Guided by the Universe's celestial might.
It weaves the threads of fate, with delicate care,
Manifesting our dreams, beyond compare.

As we send our intentions, like ripples on a pond,
The Universe receives them and responds beyond.
It aligns the stars, and shifts the tides,
Creating opportunities, where none reside.

The Universe listens, to our heart's deepest plea,
It recognizes our yearning, it longs to see,
Our dreams come alive, in brilliant array,
And so, it conspires to make a way.

With every intention, we set forth in trust,
The Universe responds, for it is just.
It sends signs and synchronicities along our path,
Guiding us closer to our heart's truest path.

Sometimes the response may be subtle and small,
A gentle nudge, a whisper in the soul's hall.

Other times, it may be grand and bold,
A manifestation of dreams, we long to behold.

But rest assured, the Universe always replies,
To our focused intentions, it never denies.
It dances with the stars, and paints the sky,
Creating a reality, where dreams can't deny.

So let us set our intentions, with unwavering belief,
And watch as the Universe brings us relief.
For in the symphony of life, we hold the baton,
And the Universe responds, with a resounding song.

With focused intentions, our dreams take flight,
As the Universe responds, with all its might.
So trust in the process, and surrender the rest,
For the Universe is listening, it knows what's best.

DREAM BIG

In the realm of dreams, where magic resides,
The Universe manifests, in wondrous strides.
It paints a canvas, with colors unseen,
Bringing our desires to life, like a dream.

Sometimes, it whispers through a gentle breeze,
Guiding us towards the path that brings us ease.
A chance encounter, with a kindred soul,
A serendipitous moment, making us whole.

Other times, it roars like a thunderous storm,
Breaking through barriers, in a powerful form.
An unexpected opportunity, knocking on the door,
Opening up new horizons, forevermore.

The Universe manifests, in signs and symbols,
A language unique, for each soul it humbles.
A shooting star streaking across the night,
Granting wishes, with celestial delight.

It weaves intricate patterns, in the tapestry of time,
Aligning the stars, in a celestial rhyme.
A synchronicity that leaves us in awe,
Connect the dots with a cosmic draw.

The Universe manifests, through the power of belief,
When we trust in the process, beyond any grief.
It brings forth abundance, in ways unforeseen,
Creating miracles, like a cosmic machine.

A job opportunity, that falls into our lap,
A serendipitous meeting, on an adventurous map.

A sudden breakthrough, after moments of despair,
The Universe manifests, showing us, it cares.

It manifests through the beauty of nature's embrace,
A breathtaking sunset, painting the sky's grace.
A blooming flower, in radiant bloom,
Reminding us, our dreams are not doomed.

The Universe manifests, through the power of love,
Bringing soulmates together, like stars above.
A love that transcends, space and time,
A bond forged in the cosmos, so sublime.

Trust in the Universe's mystical ways,
As it manifests dreams, in infinite arrays.
Through whispers and roars, signs and sync,
It brings forth our desires, in perfect sync.

For the Universe is abundant, and ever so kind,
Manifesting our dreams, with a cosmic bind.
So dream big, with unwavering belief,
And watch as the Universe responds, beyond belief.

TECHNOLOGY, FRIEND OR FOE?

In a world of cutting-edge technology's embrace,
We explore the possibilities, with a relentless chase.
It holds the power to extend our fragile time,
Unleashing a future where immortality may shine.

Through advancements in medicine, we strive,
To conquer ailments that threaten our lives.
Nanobots coursing through our veins, they roam,
Repairing damaged cells, bringing us back home.

Gene editing, a revolutionary tool in our hands,
Unlocking the secrets of our genetic strands.
CRISPR-Cas9, a precise molecular scalpel,
Correcting mutations, rewriting life's chapel.

Artificial intelligence, a marvel so grand,
With the potential to lend us a helping hand.
Machine learning algorithms, astute and wise,
Analyzing vast data, unveiling life's guise.

Virtual reality, a portal to another realm,
Where our consciousness can take the helm.
Immersed in a digital landscape, so surreal,
We transcend the limitations that we feel.

Robotics and automation, a future so bright,
With android companions to ease our plight.
From surgical precision to household chores,
Machines augment our lives, opening new doors.

Biotechnology, a realm of endless dreams,
Where synthetic organs can bridge life's seams.

Lab-grown tissues and organs, customized for all,
Reviving failing hearts, answering destiny's call.

Quantum computing, a realm of infinite might,
Harnessing quantum states, beyond our sight.
Solving complex problems, in a fraction of time,
Unleashing knowledge that was once confined.

With these advancements, our lifespans may extend,
As technology becomes our eternal friend.
But let us remember, amidst this grand pursuit,
To cherish our humanity, and life's precious fruit.

For technology alone cannot fill our souls,
It's the human connection that makes us whole.
Let's use innovation to enhance our existence,
But never forget the power of love's persistence.

So let us tread this path of progress with care,
Balancing the wonders that we create and share.
In a world where technology and life intertwine,
May we find harmony and thrive for all time.

A DANCE OF HUMANITY
& MACHINES

In a world of wires and circuits, so vast,
Where technology's shadow is ever cast,
We find solace in the warmth of connection,
Amidst the marvels of artificial perfection.

In the realm of algorithms and artificial minds,
Human connection is what truly binds.
For in the midst of this digital symphony,
It's the touch of a hand that sets us free.

In a world where screens divide our gaze,
Human connection illuminates our days.
A smile, a hug, a heartfelt conversation,
These are the keystrokes of true elation.

Amidst the noise of automation's hum,
We yearn for connection, to feel less numb.
For the soul craves the essence of another,
Embracing vulnerability, like no other.

While AI may learn and algorithms may predict,
It's the human heart that adds the missing flick.
Emotions that surge, compassion that ignites,
These are the treasures that make life so bright.

Yet let us not fear the march of technology,
For it can enhance our human connectivity.
Through screens and wires, we bridge the divide,
Extending our reach, bringing hearts side by side.

But in this dance of humanity and machine,
Let's remember the beauty that lies between.
For it's in the moments of genuine affection,
That we find the true essence of our connection.

So let us nurture the bonds we hold dear,
In this age of innovation, so crystal clear.
For technology may evolve and AI may grow,
But the power of human connection will always glow.

In the midst of technological advancements tide,
Let's cherish the connections we have inside.
A reminder that amidst the artificial gleam,
It's the human touch that makes life a dream.

ENHANCING CONNECTIVITY

In this age of marvels, where technology thrives,
It weaves a tapestry where human connection thrives.
Through wires and waves, it expands our reach,
Enhancing our connectivity, like a wondrous breach.

Social media platforms, where friends unite,
Distance collapses, regardless of the night.
We share our stories, our joys, and our pain,
Building bridges of empathy, a digital terrain.

Video calls, a lifeline across the miles,
Bringing loved ones close, with radiant smiles.
Families reunite, despite oceans apart,
Technology's embrace mends the longing heart.

Online communities, where passions align,
Kindred spirits connect; their interests entwine.
From art to sports, every niche finds its place,
Technology's embrace fosters shared space.

Collaboration blooms, in virtual realms so vast,
Innovation sparks, as ideas are amassed.
From across the globe, minds intertwine,
Technology's embrace fuels creativity's shine.

Education transcends boundaries, as knowledge flows,
Virtual classrooms open doors, where curiosity grows.
Learners connect, sharing wisdom and insight,
Technology's embrace expands horizons, day and night.

Through wearable devices, health becomes aware,
Tracking our steps, reminding us to care.

Connectivity to our bodies, a wellness guide,
Technology's embrace keeps our health in stride.

In times of crisis, technology unites,
Emergency services respond with greater might.
Alerts and updates, spreading vital information,
Technology embrace aids in our preservation.

In countless ways, technology enhances our ties,
Enriching our lives, as connectivity flies.
As long as we remember, amidst the digital sea,
Human connection is the heart, where true meaning will be.

LET'S CELEBRATE
WOMEN'S PROGRESS

In 2024, women stand tall and free,
Their progress is shining for all to see.
Compared to the 1900s, a stark divide,
Women's rights now flourish far and wide.

In the 1900s, women fought for their voice,
Struggling for suffrage, making their choice.
They rallied and marched, demanding their right,
To vote and be heard, to shine in the light.

But in 2024, women have soared,
Breaking barriers and achieving much more.
Leaders in politics, business, and science,
Their brilliance and strength reach new heights.

In politics, women now hold the key,
Leading nations with grace and empathy.
From Angela Merkel to Jacinda Ardern,
Their leadership inspires us to learn.
In the world of business, women thrive,
Creating empires, keeping dreams alive.
From Oprah Winfrey to Sheryl Sandberg,
They show us that success knows no gender.

In science and technology, women excel,
Breaking stereotypes, ringing the bell.
Katherine Johnson and Marie Curie,
Their discoveries are shaping our reality.

In sports, women dominate the field,

Their skills and prowess refuse to yield.
Serena Williams and Simone Biles,
Their achievements leave us in smiles.

But beyond these examples, let's not forget,
The progress made by women in every aspect.
From education to healthcare, from art to law,
Women's contributions leave us in awe.

In 2024, women have prospered indeed,
Their journey far from over, but they succeed.
With each passing year, they break the mold,
Empowering generations, making history unfold.

So let us celebrate the progress made,
And continue to support their crusade.
For in the status of women, we find,
A brighter future for all humankind.

SHATTERING GLASS CEILINGS

In the realm of science and technology's might,
Women have shone with their brilliant light.
Their discoveries and innovations profound,
Have shaped our reality, breaking new ground.

Marie Curie, a pioneer in her own right,
Discovered radioactivity, shining so bright.
Her work with radium and polonium's grace,
Revolutionized science in the atomic space.

Rosalind Franklin, an unsung hero of DNA,
Captured the X-ray diffraction's display.
Her image of the double helix structure,
Laid the foundation for genetic adventure.

Hedy Lamarr, an actress with a brilliant mind,
Invented frequency hopping, a gem to find.
Her invention paved the way for modern Wi-Fi,
A technological wonder, reaching the sky.

Ada Lovelace, the world's first programmer,
Conceptualized algorithms, a true innovator.
Her work on Charles Babbage's Analytical Engine,
Laid the groundwork for computers we now deem.

Now let's turn our gaze to the world of business,
Where women have risen, their success conspicuous.
Indra Nooyi, a trailblazer in PepsiCo's reign,
As CEO, she led with strategic gain.

Sheryl Sandberg, Facebook's COO,
Empowered women with her book's value.

Her message of leaning in and leadership,
Inspired countless women to reach their zenith.

In politics, women have made their mark,
Leading nations, creating a lasting spark.
Angela Merkel, Germany's Chancellor strong,
Guided her country through challenges, righting wrongs.

Jacinda Ardern, New Zealand's Prime Minister,
Led with compassion, a visionary enabler.
Her response to tragedy, a shining example,
Of empathy and strength, a leader so ample.

These women, among many others we revere,
Have shattered glass ceilings, making it clear.
That in science, technology, business, and politics,
Women's contributions are vital and iconic.

Their discoveries and leadership pave the way,
For a future where gender won't lead astray.
Let us celebrate these women who inspire,
And continue supporting their dreams set afire.

VIRTUES

In the realm of virtues, let us wander,
Setting our minds on things truly grand.
Wisdom, the beacon that guides our path,
With knowledge and insight, we shall expand.

In pursuit of wisdom, let us seek,
To understand the world's mysteries deep.
Like Socrates, who questioned with grace,
Uncovering truths that were buried, so steep.

Next, self-control, a fortress strong,
Resisting temptations that may arise.
Like Buddha, who found inner peace,
By taming desires, he reached the skies.

Justice, the pillar of a noble society,
Where fairness and equality prevail.
Like Martin Luther King Jr., who fought,
For civil rights, his voice never failed.

Courage, the flame that ignites our souls,
To face challenges with bravery untold.
Like Malala, who stood for girls' education,
Defying oppression, her story unfolds.

With these virtues, our minds aligned,
Unquestionably good, they shine so brightly.
Let us strive for wisdom, self-control,
Justice, and courage, in every life's fight.

For in setting our minds upon these ideals,
We shape a world where goodness prevails.

And like the heroes who came before,
We'll leave a legacy that never fails.

CREATING A WORLD
BEYOND COMPARE

In a world where darkness may prevail,
Let us embark on a noble tale.
A story of hope, where goodness thrives,
Where compassion and love forever survive.

With hearts aligned, let's paint a new dawn,
A canvas of kindness, where hate is withdrawn.
For in the depths of our souls, we hold the key,
To create a world where goodness is free.

Let's plant the seeds of empathy and care,
Nurturing compassion, spreading it everywhere.
Like a ripple in a pond, let it expand,
Touching hearts, uniting hand in hand.

In this world, let justice be our guide,
Where equality and fairness coincide.
Breaking chains of oppression, setting people free,
For in unity, we find true harmony.

Courage, a beacon, let it light our way,
To face adversity, come what may.
With unwavering resolve, let's stand tall,
Confronting challenges, breaking down walls.

Together, let's build a legacy that won't fade,
Where goodness prevails, where memories are made.
A legacy of love, kindness, and grace,
That transcends time, leaving an eternal embrace.

So let us strive, let us dare,
To create a world that's beyond compare.
Where goodness prevails, and darkness subsides,
Leaving a legacy that never fails, forever abides.

LET GO OF CONTROL

When inner blockages hold you tight,
And life's flow seems out of sight,
Release the chains that bind your soul,
Discover the path that makes you whole.

To align with the flow, let go of control,
Embrace the uncertainty that life may unfold.
For in surrender, you find true release,
And inner blockages begin to cease.

Stay present and in the moment's embrace,
Amidst the chaos, find your inner grace.
When things don't go as you desire,
Seek the lessons and let go of the fire.

For life's twists and turns are meant to teach,
To guide you towards the truths you seek.
Embrace the challenges, learn from the strife,
And align with the rhythm of your own life.

In the stillness of each passing breath,
Find solace amidst the chaos and unrest.
Let go of worries that burden your mind,
And trust in the journey, one step at a time.

For the flow of life is ever-changing,
Adapt and evolve, without hesitating.
Stay present, grounded, and aware,
In the face of challenges, show resilience and care.

Let gratitude be your guiding light,
Even when the path may not seem right.

Release the need for things to align,
And let the universe's plan intertwine.

In the dance of life, embrace the unknown,
With an open heart, let your spirit be shown.
Release inner blockages, let your soul be free,
And align with the flow of your destiny.

SEEKING & FINDING SOLACE

In the midst of chaos and unrest,
Where worries and anxieties infest,
There lies a place of solace, serene,
A refuge where tranquility can be seen.

Amidst the storm that rages on,
Seek solace where peace is drawn.
In nature's embrace, find your retreat,
Where harmony and stillness meet.

Beneath the canopy of trees so tall,
Let their whispers calm your soul.
Feel the gentle breeze upon your face,
As it carries away worries, leaving no trace.

In the vastness of the ocean's expanse,
Find solace in its rhythmic dance.
Let the waves wash away your fears,
And cleanse your spirit, wiping away tears.

In the quiet corners of a sacred space,
Find solace in stillness, embrace the grace.
Meditate, breathe, and let go,
Allow inner peace to bloom and grow.

Seek solace in the company of loved ones,
Where genuine connections are spun.
In their support and understanding, find,
A refuge that eases the troubled mind.

Through art and music, find solace's gate,
Express your emotions, let creativity resonate.

In the strokes of a brush or the notes of a song,
Discover solace where you truly belong.
Find solace in the pages of a book,
Where stories can travel and overlook,
The chaos and unrest that surrounds,
Immerse yourself in tales profound.

In acts of kindness, find solace's embrace,
Lend a helping hand, bring smiles to a face.
For in giving, you receive solace profound,
In the unity of compassion, peace is found.

So amidst the chaos and unrest,
Seek solace, let it be your quest.
For in the moments of quiet and peace,
You'll find the strength to face, to release.

RELAXING INTO
THE PRESENT MOMENT

In the realm of learning's embrace,
Where resistance finds its place,
We seek the path to tranquil shores,
Where acceptance blooms and soars.

With open hearts, we start to learn,
To let go of all those churns,
Emotional tides we gently release,
Finding solace and inner peace.

On the physical plane, we explore,
Meditations that heal and restore,
Releasing tension with each breath,
Finding freedom from life's duress.

Energetic waves, we navigate,
Releasing blockages that stagnate,
With mindfulness, we flow and mend,
Allowing energy to transcend.

Through practice and dedication,
We find the key to liberation,
Relaxing into each present moment,
With gratitude, our hearts are potent.

Learning to let go, we find the way,
To embrace acceptance day by day,
In the dance of life, we find our groove,
Letting resistance dissolve and move.

So, let us journey on this quest,
To release what no longer serves us best,
Learning practices that set us free,
To relax into acceptance, effortlessly.

In this realm of learning and meditation,
We find the path to liberation,
Embracing each moment as it comes,
With open hearts, we become as one.

EMBRACING EACH MOMENT

In the realm of time's embrace,
Where moments weave their delicate lace,
There lies wisdom, pure and true,
In embracing each moment, old and new.

For in the present, life unfolds,
A tapestry of stories yet untold,
Each fleeting second, a precious gem,
To cherish and hold close to them.

The past, it fades into the mist,
The future, yet a gentle twist,
But the present, oh, it holds the key,
To unlock the beauty that's meant to be.

In each breath, a universe resides,
A symphony of moments, collides,
The laughter, tears, and all between,
The richness of life, yet unseen.

Embracing each moment, we find,
A sanctuary for the heart and mind,
For worries fade and fears subside,
In the beauty of now, we truly reside.

No longer burdened by regret's weight,
Nor anxious thoughts that anticipate,
We dance with grace, in harmony,
With the rhythm of life's symphony.

In joy, we savor every morsel,
In sadness, we find solace and wrestle,

For every moment holds its own grace,
A precious gift, in time and space.

So let us pause, and take a breath,
Embrace each moment, beyond life's breadth,
For in the present, we truly live,
A gift of presence, we freely give.

In the tapestry of life's grand art,
We find the wisdom to play our part,
Embracing each moment, as it comes,
We discover the beauty that truly hums.

So let us cherish this sacred dance,
Embrace each moment, take a chance,
For in the present, we find our way,
To live fully, in each passing day.

CHOOSE GRATITUDE

In the realm of our inner mind,
A tumultuous dance we find,
An antagonistic relationship with life,
A constant struggle, a cause for strife.

But in the depths of this inner war,
Lies a truth worth exploring, and much more,
For when we step out of negativity's hold,
A transformation occurs; a story unfolds.

In the practical realm of daily life,
Insights down to earth can ease the strife,
Embrace the beauty of each passing day,
Let go of worries, let go of dismay.

Find solace in the simple joys,
A gentle breeze, a child's playful noise,
Embrace the present, let go of the past,
Unburden the mind, let peace amass.

Pause and breathe, in moments of stress,
Find stillness within, a moment to bless,
For in the stillness, clarity resides,
A calmness of spirit, where joy abides.

Choose gratitude as your guiding light,
In every challenge, find a glimmer bright,
Shift your perspective, see the silver lining,
And watch as positivity begins shining.

Eckhart's wisdom reminds us all,
To rise above the struggles, big and small,

Embrace life's journey with an open heart,
And let negativity slowly depart.

So let us seek the source of light,
Step out of darkness, embrace what's right,
For in this shift, a new world awaits,
Where joy and peace forever resonates.

LIVING IN A BEAUTIFUL STATE

In a world of infinite choices, we stand,
At the crossroads, with decisions in our hand.
To live in a beautiful state, we must decide,
To embrace gratitude and let our spirits glide.

Every single cell in our body, a miracle in itself,
A symphony of life, that we often overlook and shelf.
Let's be thankful for each breath, each beat of our heart,
And cherish the gift of health, never to depart.

In a beautiful state, we find joy in simple things,
The laughter of a child, the melody that nature sings.
The blooming of a flower, the sunrise in the sky,
Moments that bring peace, as time goes by.

To live in a beautiful state, we choose peace,
Letting go of worries, allowing our souls to release.
Finding solace in stillness, in the depths of our mind,
A tranquil oasis, where contentment we find.

Decisions shape our destiny, our path forward,
Choosing a beautiful state, our spirits soar and onward.
So let us decide to live with gratitude and grace,
In a state of beauty, embracing life's every embrace.

DECISIONS HOLD POWER

In the realm of choices, our destiny unfolds,
Each decision we make, our future molds.
For in the hands of choice, our path takes shape,
Leading us to triumphs or lessons to escape.

Decisions hold power, like a guiding star,
They shape our journey, no matter how far.
With every crossroad, we stand and reflect,
Choosing our direction, with intellect.

Simple things bring joy, in everyday life,
Like a warm embrace, erasing all strife.
A gentle breeze against a summer's cheek,
Or the laughter of loved ones, tender and meek.

The scent of blooming flowers, in fields so vast,
Or the taste of sweet fruits, a flavor that lasts.
A sunrise painting the sky with hues so bright,
Or a starry night, filling our hearts with delight.

The touch of soft sand beneath our feet,
Or the sound of raindrops, creating a rhythmic beat.
A book that captivates, transporting us away,
Or a heartfelt conversation, where words gently sway.

In decisions we find power to shape our fate,
To choose love over hate and not hesitate.
To embrace opportunities with open arms,
And learn from the failures, like life's alarms.

So let us cherish the simple joys each day,
And make decisions that light our way.

For in shaping our destiny, we hold the key,
To a life filled with purpose and joyful glee.

236

THE ART OF FULFILLMENT

In the realm of science, achievement takes flight,
With diligent minds, seeking wisdom's light.
Through research and discovery, we advance,
Unraveling mysteries, taking a chance.

In labs and equations, we strive for progress,
Pushing boundaries, we never digress.
From theories to inventions, we forge ahead,
Creating a legacy, where dreams are spread.

But beyond the realm of science, lies an art,
The art of fulfillment, where passions impart.
It's not just about the goals we achieve,
But finding purpose, so our souls can believe.

For achievement alone cannot bring us peace,
It's the art of fulfillment that brings release.
It's in the moments of joy and connection,
Where we find contentment, a soul's reflection.

The art of fulfillment lies in simple things,
Like a child's laughter or the joy that it brings.
Or a heartfelt conversation with a dear friend,
Where time stands still, and love knows no end.

It's in the beauty of nature, so grand,
Where awe and wonder, like a symphony, expand.
A sunset's embrace, painting the sky,
Or a starry night, where dreams can fly.

The art of fulfillment lies in gratitude,
In counting blessings, with a humble attitude.

Finding meaning in service, in giving back,
To make a difference, on the right track.

So let us embrace both science and art,
For achievement and fulfillment, they impart.
With knowledge and purpose, hand in hand,
We can shape a future, where dreams expand.

EMPOWERING EMOTIONS

In the realm of emotions, power resides,
Where strength and courage within us abides.
Empowering emotions, they light up our soul,
Igniting a fire, making us whole.

When love takes hold, it's a force so divine,
A feeling so pure, like a sparkling wine.
It lifts us up, gives us wings to fly,
Bringing warmth and joy, as time passes by.

In the face of fear, we find bravery's might,
A surge of courage, like a beacon of light.
It pushes us forward, to conquer our doubts,
Unlocking our potential, breaking through clouds.

Hope is a flame that never burns out,
A flicker of faith, dispelling any doubt.
It fuels our dreams, keeps our spirits high,
Guiding us through darkness, towards the sky.

Compassion, a virtue that touches the soul,
A selfless act, making others feel whole.
A helping hand, a comforting embrace,
Empathy in action, leaving a trace.

Happiness, a state that uplifts our being,
A sense of contentment, so freeing.
It's in the laughter, the smiles we share,
A moment of bliss, beyond compare.

Courage, resilience, and confidence, too,
Emotions that empower, helping us breakthrough.

They fuel determination, ignite our drive,
Pushing us forward, helping us thrive.

So let us embrace these empowering emotions,
Harness their power, like magical potions.
For in their presence, we find our strength,
Creating a life of purpose, to any length.

SOARING TO NEW HEIGHTS

In the journey of life, emotions unfold,
Empowering our hearts, making us bold.
They guide our steps, through joy and strife,
Unleashing our potential, igniting our life.

Hope, a beacon in the darkest night,
A glimmer of light, shining so bright.
It whispers of possibilities yet to be,
Filling our hearts with endless glee.

It lifts us from despair, when all seems lost,
Infusing our souls with strength and exhaust.
With hope in our hearts, we rise above,
Conquering challenges, fueled by love.

Love, a symphony of emotions untold,
A feeling so pure, like molten gold.
It's a warm embrace, that makes us whole,
A connection that touches the depths of our soul.

Love feels like a gentle breeze on a summer's day,
Caressing our hearts in the most tender way.
It's a sanctuary, a refuge from the storm,
A bond that keeps us safe and warm.

It's the laughter that echoes, filling the air,
The tender moments we willingly share.
Love is a language, spoken without words,
A melody that lingers, like singing birds.

Empowering emotions, they shape our path,
Gifting us strength, in moments of wrath.

Through hope and love, we find our way,
Transforming our lives, day by day.

So let us embrace these emotions dear,
For they guide us through both joy and fear.
With hope as our compass, and love as our guide,
We soar to new heights, with hearts open wide.

DISEMPOWERING EMOTIONS

In shadows of doubt, disempowerment resides,
A fallacy that lingers, where hope subsides.
These emotions deceive, leading us astray,
Binding our spirit, in a web of dismay.

Fear, a master of illusion and deceit,
Constricts our hearts, making us retreat.
It whispers of failure, with every step we take,
Leaving us paralyzed, afraid to awake.

Regret, a haunting ghost of the past,
Weighs us down, with memories amassed.
It buries our dreams, in a graveyard of remorse,
Leaving us trapped, with no chance for recourse.

Self-doubt, a relentless voice in our mind,
Undermines our worth, leaving us confined.
It questions our abilities, our every move,
Leaving us stagnant, unable to improve.

Disempowerment emotions, they hold us back,
Painting our world in shades of black.
They blind us to possibilities, cloud our view,
Preventing us from embracing something new.

But let us not succumb to their deceit,
For within us lies the power to defeat.
We can rise above, like a phoenix from the ashes,
Unleashing our potential, breaking free from these clashes.
Choose courage over fear, to forge a new way,
Leave regret behind, embrace a brighter day.

Believe in yourself, banish self-doubt's plight,
And reclaim your power, with all your might.

For disempowerment emotions, though they may try,
Not extinguish the fire, that burns inside.
With resilience and strength, we shall prevail,
As we rewrite our story and set sail.

So let us cast aside the fallacy of disempowerment,
And embrace the truth of our own empowerment.
For within us lies a power, strong and true,
To overcome any obstacle and start anew.

THE KEY TO OVERCOMING DISEMPOWERMENT

In the depths of our souls, disempowering emotions reside,
They bind our spirit, leaving us confined.
They whisper of doubt and sow seeds of fear,
Leaving us stagnant, unable to steer.

Like chains that weigh heavy upon our hearts,
Disempowering emotions tear us apart.
They hold us back from reaching our true potential,
Leaving us trapped in a cycle, never transcendental.

But amidst this darkness, there lies a key,
A key to unlock the shackles and set us free.
It is the power of self-awareness, shining bright,
Guiding us towards a path of inner light.

To overcome disempowering emotions, we must first see,
Acknowledge their presence and let them be.
For in awareness lies the power to choose,
To transcend the limitations, and refuse.

With self-compassion, we can heal the wounds,
Embracing our imperfections, like delicate blooms.
For it is acceptable that true strength is found,
And in vulnerability, our spirit is unbound.

Seeking support, we find solace in connection,
Surrounding ourselves with love and affection.
Through empathy and understanding, we rise,
Nurturing our spirit, like butterflies in the skies.

Self-reflection becomes our guiding light,
Examining our thoughts, shining truth so bright.
Challenging the disempowering beliefs we hold,
Replacing them with empowering stories, bold.

Mindfulness becomes our faithful companion,
Grounding us in the present, like a tranquil canyon.
It anchors us amidst the storms that may arise,
Allowing us to respond, rather than agonize.

And as we journey on this path of liberation,
We discover the strength within our true foundation.
No longer bound by disempowering emotions' sway,
We reclaim our power, and live life our own way.

So let us unlock the chains that bind,
And release the spirit that's confined.
For in the depths of our being, we hold the key,
To overcome disempowering emotions and truly be free.

FOCUS AND ENERGY

In the realm of thoughts and dreams,
Truth whispers on silent streams.
Where focus goes, energy follows,
A power within us that truly hallowed.

For when we direct our gaze with intent,
Energy surges, it becomes potent.
Like a flowing river, strong and steady,
Our focus shapes our reality, ready.

In every moment, a choice is made,
To let our focus wander or be swayed.
But when we recognize the power we hold,
Our dreams and desires begin to unfold.

With a focused mind, we manifest,
The energy we truly invest.
For what we give our attention and time,
Grows and expands, reaching sublime.

If we dwell on negativity, it will grow,
Feeding on our thoughts, it will sow.
But if we shift our focus to the positive,
Energy flows, and we become more alive.

In the face of challenges, we find,
That where focus goes, solutions unwind.
With determination and a clear vision,
Our energy aligns, a powerful mission.

So let us choose wisely, where we direct,
The focus of our mind, the thoughts we select.

For in this awareness, a door opens wide,
To a world of possibilities, where dreams reside.

With focused energy, we create our fate,
Manifesting dreams, it's never too late.
Believe in the power that lies within,
And watch as your reality begins to spin.

So remember, dear soul, as you go,
Where focus goes, energy will flow.
Harness the power, embrace the sublime,
And create a life that's truly divine.

THE BEAUTY OF INTENTION

In the realm of purpose and intent,
A beauty unfolds, like nature's scent.
When we direct our gaze with clarity,
The world reveals its true majesty.

Imagine the artist, brush in hand,
Creating a masterpiece, a work so grand.
With each intentional stroke and hue,
A canvas comes alive, a vision true.

Or think of the athlete, focused and strong,
Determined to prove their abilities belong.
With every stride and leap in their quest,
They surpassed limits, reaching their best.

In relationships, when our gaze is clear,
We see beauty in those we hold dear.
With love and kindness, we nurture and grow,
Creating bonds that only deepen and glow.

In the realm of knowledge and exploration,
Our focused gaze reveals revelation.
With curious minds and open hearts,
We uncover wisdom, piece by part.

Consider the inventor, driven by a dream,
Their intent fuels innovation's gleam.
With focused minds and relentless will,
They bring forth inventions that thrill.

In the pursuit of dreams and aspirations,
Our intent guides us through life's transformations.

With purposeful actions, we manifest,
The beauty of a life truly blessed.

So let us direct our gaze with intent,
Embrace the beauty that lies in every event.
For when we focus on what truly matters,
Life's wonders unfold, like a symphony that scatters.

In the beauty of intention, we find,
A world that is rich, and one of a kind.
With every thought and action, we choose,
We shape a reality that's ours to infuse.
Cherish the power of intent's embrace,
And marvel at the beauty it helps create.
For when we direct our gaze with clarity,
The world reveals its true magnanimity.

A WORLD FILL OF WONDER

In the depths of curiosity's embrace,
A world of wonders awaits a magical space.
With a curious mind and an open heart,
We embark on a journey, a transformative art.

In the realm of knowledge, we dare to explore,
Uncovering secrets never seen before.
With questions as our compass, we set sail,
Seeking truths that our curious minds unveil.

With every step we take, our intent prevails,
Guiding us through life's transformative trails.
Through trials and challenges, we persevere,
For our curious minds hold no fear.

In the realms of science, we seek to know,
Unraveling mysteries that constantly grow.
With an open heart, we embrace the unknown,
Discovering truths that have yet to be shown.

In the arts, our curious minds find solace,
Seeking beauty and meaning with every stroke of a brush.
With an open heart, we let creativity flow,
Transforming emotions into a vibrant tableau.

Through the corridors of history, we wander,
Curiosity as our guide, our intent as a ponder.
With open hearts, we learn from the past,
Shaping a future that will forever last.

In the realm of relationships, we delve,
Curiosity and openness, the stories we shall unveil.

With an intent to understand and connect,
We build bridges of love, never to neglect.

With a curious mind and an open heart,
We navigate life's labyrinth, a transformative art.
Guided by intent, we find our purpose and way,
Unveiling the beauty that unfolds every day.

So let us nurture our curiosity's flame,
And let our open hearts be the compass that remains.
For with intent as our guide through life's transformation,
We uncover a world filled with wonder and elation.

RECONCILIATION AND FORGIVENESS

In the realm of hearts, where wounds reside,
Reconciliation and forgiveness abide.
They hold the power to heal and restore,
Unleashing a spirit, resilient to the core.

When conflicts arise, and friendships fade,
Reconciliation paves a path to serenade.
It bridges the gaps, where understanding lacks,
Mending broken bonds, bringing peace back.

Like a gentle rain, forgiveness descends,
Washing away resentment, making amends.
It lifts the burden from a heavy heart,
Allowing the spirit to soar and restart.

In the aftermath of wars and strife,
Reconciliation breathes new life.
From Rwanda's scarred land, a story unfolds,
As enemies became friends, a tale untold.

In South Africa, a nation's soul revived,
Through forgiveness, wounds were deprived.
Nelson Mandela's embrace, a symbol so grand,
Uniting a nation, with peace at hand.

Within families, forgiveness finds its place,
Healing generations, leaving no trace.
Siblings who once quarreled, now embrace,
Reconciliation's power, their love to embrace.

In personal realms, forgiveness sets us free,
Releasing the shackles that bind you and me.
Through understanding and empathy's embrace,
A wounded spirit finds solace and grace.

Forgiveness is not weakness, but strength untold,
It mends the broken, makes hearts unfold.
Reconciliation, a bridge to unite,
Transforming darkness into radiant light.

So let us strive for reconciliation's embrace,
And let forgiveness shine in every space.
For in the healing of wounds, we find release,
And our spirits soar, embracing inner peace.

GIVE ME SOME LOVE

Give me some love, give me some love,
Because I need it, because I want it.
In the depths of my being, hunger stirs,
Yearning for love's touch, as my heart defers.

With each word, a plea reverberates,
An anthem of desire that resonates.
For love is the elixir that fuels our fire,
Igniting the soul with a burning desire.

Give me some love, give me some love,
Because I need it, because I want it.
In the darkest nights, when shadows loom,
Love's gentle glow can chase away the gloom.

It is the warmth that softens the coldest hearts,
A balm that heals, when life tears us apart.
In love's tender embrace, we find solace and peace,
A sanctuary where all troubles cease.

Give me some love, give me some love,
Because I need it, because I want it.
For in love's presence, we find our worth,
A sense of belonging, a rebirth.

It is the laughter that dances upon our lips,
The gentle touch of fingertips.
Love's symphony, an eternal song,
With every verse, our spirits grow strong.

Give me some love, give me some love,
Because I need it, because I want it.

Let love be the compass that guides us through,
In its embrace, our dreams come true.

So let the words resound, let the plea be heard,
For love is the language in which hearts are stirred.
Give me some love, and watch me soar,
For love's embrace, I forever adore.

I AM A SPECIAL BEING

In the tapestry of life, a special being,
Who weaves serenity from chaos, gently intervening.
With a touch so gentle, calmness is born,
Transforming the storms into tranquil morn.

From the depths of turmoil, you summon peace,
A master of stillness, where worries cease.
Silence finds solace in your serene embrace,
As you navigate the currents with grace.

In the quietude, your essence blooms,
Radiating energy, dispelling all gloom.
A vessel of tranquility, pure and bright,
Harnessing the power of stillness, your guiding light.

With every breath, you harmonize the soul,
Embracing the moments that make us whole.
In the stillness, you find your truest form,
Pure energy, vibrant and warm.

Through your presence, the world finds repose,
As you weave tranquility wherever you go.
A beacon of serenity, a guiding star,
Leading others to the peaceful shores afar.

In the chaos of life, you stand tall and strong,
A testament to the beauty of staying calm.
For in your being, a special gift resides,
Transforming the world with your peaceful strides.

So embrace your essence, dear special being,
For in your presence, serenity is freeing.

Silence, calmness, and stillness your art,
A masterpiece of peace, a reflection of your heart.

258

Silence, calmness, and stillness your art,
A masterpiece of peace, a reflection of your heart.

THE QUALITY OF MY EMOTIONS

In the realm of existence, a truth unfolds,
The quality of your life, in emotions it holds.
For you are not the thoughts that come and go,
Nor the fleeting feelings that ebb and flow.

You are the observer, a witness to it all,
Watching the emotions rise and fall.
In the depths of your being, a serene space,
Unaffected by the chaos, a stillness you embrace.

Your life's canvas painted with vibrant hues,
Reflecting the emotions, both joy and blues.
But you, dear soul, remain steadfast and true,
The observer within, untouched, never askew.

In moments of bliss, your spirit soars high,
Like a bird in the sky, reaching for the sky.
You witness the joy, let it dance and play,
Knowing it shall pass, like a fleeting ray.

In moments of sorrow, your heart may ache,
Yet you stand firm, never to break.
For you are not defined by the tears you shed,
But by the resilience, rising from within instead.

The quality of your life, a reflection it bears,
Of the emotions you choose the love you share.
In the face of challenges, you find your grace,
Guided by the observer, a steady pace.

So remember, dear one, in this wondrous dance,
You are not the emotions, but the observer's glance.

Embrace the highs and lows, the ebb and flow,
For the quality of your life, in emotions it shall show.

Through the tapestry of feelings, you navigate,
With wisdom and clarity, you illuminate.
For you are the observer, a beacon of light,
Guiding your life's journey, shining so bright.

THE OBSERVER,
FINDING THE TRUTH

In the grand theater of life, there's a role to play,
As the observer, you guide the way.
Amidst the chaos and the emotional tide,
You stand as a witness, undeterred and wide-eyed.

Through the labyrinth of feelings, you tread,
With a curious mind and a heart widespread.
You watch as emotions rise and fall,
Like waves crashing against an eternal wall.

As an observer, you hold a sacred space,
To witness the emotions, with gentle grace.
You don't resist or cling to any state,
But embrace them all, without judgment or debate.

In moments of joy, you bask in the light,
Savoring beauty, pure delight.
You let the laughter fill your very core,
And relish in the happiness, forevermore.

When sorrow visits, you lend a compassionate ear,
Listening to the whispers of pain and fear.
You acknowledge the tears that freely flow,
And offer solace, a gentle presence to show.

As the observer, you navigate the stormy seas,
Guiding the ship through emotional unease.
You keep the compass steady, the sails unfurled,
Finding balance in chaos, a stabilizing world.

You know that feelings, like passing clouds, will drift,
But the observer remains ever swift.
You hold the power to choose your response,
To embrace the emotions and let them dance.

Through the highs and lows, you find your way,
Observing the thoughts and feelings that sway.
You cultivate awareness, a mindful gaze,
And navigate through life's intricate maze.

The significance of the observer, you see,
It is in finding the truth of who you can be.
To witness the emotions, both gentle and fierce,
And find the wisdom within, ever so clear.

So, embrace your role as the observer profound,
In this journey of life, where emotions abound.
Navigate with grace through the vast unknown,
For the observer within is your guiding star.

SELF-MASTERY

In the grand theater of life, a role so profound,
The observer takes center stage, where wisdom is found.
With eyes wide open, and a heart so keen,
The observer creates the master of their own scene.

Like an artist with a canvas, blank and pure,
The observer chooses what they will endure.
They paint their reality with thoughts and intention,
Crafting a masterpiece, a personal invention.

In the realm of emotions, they hold the reins,
Choosing which ones to amplify, which to restrain.
They embrace love's warmth, its gentle caress,
And release the grip of anger's distress.

When faced with challenges, they find strength,
To transform adversity into a journey of length.
They choose resilience, in the face of strife,
And turn obstacles into steppingstones of life.

The observer knows the power of their mind,
To shape their world, both gentle and kind.
With thoughts as seeds, they sow what they desire,
Creating a life that sets their soul on fire.

They choose forgiveness over bitterness and hate,
Releasing the burden, setting themselves straight.
With compassion as their guide, they lend a helping hand,
Creating a ripple effect across the land.

Self-mastery, the observer seeks to attain,
To understand their essence, their inner domain.

They dive deep within, exploring their truth,
Uncovering treasures, embracing their youth.

Through self-reflection, they gain clarity,
Recognizing patterns, breaking free from disparity.
They cultivate mindfulness, a presence so serene,
Steering their ship through waters unforeseen.

The observer understands the power of choice,
To create a life that resonates with their voice.
They manifest dreams, with unwavering belief,
And navigate the currents, finding solace and relief.
In the grand theater of life, the observer stands tall,
Creating their story, embracing the call.
With each breath they take, they shape their fate,
Guided by wisdom, they transcend and elevate.

So, step into the role of the observer within,
Embrace the power to create, to begin.
Choose your thoughts, your actions, your path,
And behold the masterpiece of your life's aftermath.

OUR LIFE SUSTAINING BREATH

In the rhythm of life, a precious gift we possess,
A tool of existence, the breath, we cannot repress.
With each inhale and exhale, a symphony of grace,
The importance of our breath, let us embrace.

Through the breath, emotions find their release,
A gentle whisper, a sigh, a moment of peace.
In times of anger, when tempers ignite,
The breath brings calmness, a soothing light.

When sadness envelops, like a heavy cloak,
The breath offers solace, a ray of hope.
Inhaling the essence of love, exhaling the pain,
The breath carries us through the darkest of rain.

In moments of fear, when shadows loom,
Breath brings courage, dispelling the gloom.
With each steady inhale, strength we reclaim,
Exhaling doubt, embracing a fearless domain.

Breath teaches us the art of presence,
To be here and now, in every essence.
In the chaos of life, a moment to pause,
The breath grounds us, connecting with our cause.

With each mindful breath, we find clarity,
The fog of confusion lifts, revealing reality.
In the face of challenges, both big and small,
The breath empowers us to stand tall.

Compassion flows through the breath's gentle flow,
A bridge to connect, a kindness to bestow.

In understanding the struggles that others face,
The breath guides us to respond with grace.

In the grand tapestry of humanity's plight,
Breathing unites us, a universal light.
From the newborn's cry to the elder's sigh,
The breath unifies, transcending the why.

So, let us honor the breath, a treasure untold,
A tool to control, our emotions to behold.
With each inhale and exhale, let us seek,
The power within, the breath's mystique.

For in the breath lies our strength and our peace,
A guiding force, that will never cease.
Through the ebb and flow of life's ceaseless tide,
The breath carries us with love as our guide.

I AM THE MASTER OF MY MIND

In the depths of my being, a power untold,
I am the master of my mind, the captain of my soul.
With every thought, I shape my destiny,
A creator of dreams, a vessel of clarity.

When doubt clouds my path, like a stormy sea,
I steer my ship, with unwavering certainty.
Through turbulent waters, I find my way,
Guided by the compass of my will each day.

In moments of weakness, when shadows descend,
I rise from within, my spirit to mend.
I am the master of my mind, strong and bold,
Harnessing courage, a story yet untold.

In the face of adversity, I stand tall,
Defying limitations, breaking down the wall.
With resilience as my armor, I forge ahead,
Unleashing my potential, no longer misled.

When fear whispers, "Retreat, don't dare to try,"
I silenced its voice, with a resolute reply.
For I am the captain of my soul's great ship,
Navigating through challenges with a steadfast grip.

In the realm of possibilities, I dare to explore,
Unleashing creativity, forever wanting more.
With every stroke of inspiration's brush,
I paint my dreams, a masterpiece to rush.

When darkness threatens to dim my inner light,
I ignite the flame, burning ever bright.

I am the master of my mind, the keeper of fire,
Fueling my passions, reaching higher and higher.

Through self-discovery, I find my true voice,
Embracing authenticity, making my choice.
For I am the captain of my soul's grand fleet,
Sailing towards purpose, with passion as my beat.

In the symphony of life, I compose my own tune,
Harmonizing dreams, creating a celestial boon.
With every decision, I shape my own fate,
Writing a narrative that's uniquely great.

So, let the world bear witness to my control,
As I steer my ship with a determined soul.
I am the master of my mind and captain of my soul,
A force to be reckoned with, forever whole.

REAL ESTATE IS A CONTACT SPORT

In the realm of real estate, a contact sport is deemed,
Where victories are found, not just in plans and dreams.
For if you wish to flourish, to rise and to stand tall,
Contacts are the lifeblood, the key to conquer all.

In this game of transactions, where fortunes are at stake,
Contacts pave the pathway, their value none can break.
With each connection forged, a door swings open wide,
Opportunities arise, as fortunes coincide.

Imagine a realtor, with charisma and grace,
Whose network extends far, reaching every place.
They mingle with investors, with buyers and with sellers,
Their contacts are like gold, the envy of their fellows.

They attend networking events, shaking hands with might,
Exchanging cards and stories, under starry night.
From boardrooms to luncheons, they navigate the crowd,
Building bridges of trust, where success is allowed.

For a real estate agent, connections are the key,
To unlock the doors of possibility.
They know the developers, the lenders, and the brokers,
Across cities and states, their reach never falters.

Take, for instance, a young couple seeking a home,
Lost in a sea of options, feeling all alone.
But through a contact's referral, they find a guiding hand,
A realtor with expertise, who helps them understand.

Or picture an investor, with dreams of real estate,
Seeking lucrative deals, where profits elevate.

Through a contact's introduction, they find a hidden gem,
A property ripe for growth, a seller's loss, their win.

In this contact sport, persistence is the key,
For every unanswered call, brings you closer, you'll see.
It's a numbers game, where rejection's just a sign,
To keep pushing forward, to make more contacts, divine.

So, if you wish to conquer, to thrive and to succeed,
Real estate as a contact sport, you must believe.
For in the realm of properties, fortunes can be made,
But without the right connections, dreams may start to fade.

Remember, in this game, it's contacts that empower,
To navigate the market, to ascend and tower.
So, build your network wisely, seek out new alliances,
For in the world of real estate, contacts are the prizes.

RIGHTEOUSNESS IS BEAUTIFUL

In the realm of righteousness, beauty finds its place,
A virtue that shines with celestial grace.
For in the depths of goodness, where noble hearts reside,
True beauty blossoms, with a radiant stride.

Behold the righteous soul, whose actions speak aloud,
They walk the path of honor, a beacon in the crowd.
Through acts of kindness, they paint a world so fair,
A masterpiece of love, with compassion beyond compare.

Like gentle rain, they quench the thirsty ground,
Offering solace to the lost, the broken, and the bound.
They lend a helping hand, without seeking praise or fame,
Their selflessness deeds an ode to righteousness' name.

In the face of injustice, they stand tall and brave,
Defending truth and fairness, their banners gently wave.
They champion equality, where all are seen as one,
Embracing diversity, until the battle's won.

Consider the advocate, fighting for the voiceless,
Their passion ignites change, their courage ever priceless.
They challenge the oppressor, with unwavering might,
Seeking justice and freedom, in the name of what is right.

Or witness the mentor, guiding the lost and young,
With wisdom like a river, from which knowledge is sprung.
They nurture minds and spirits, with patience and with care,
Illuminating paths, where dreams can freely dare.

In the realm of righteousness, beauty takes its form,
Where empathy and grace weather the darkest storm.

It's not in outward appearances, but in the soul's embrace,
That righteousness reveals its loveliness and grace.

For true beauty lies within, in acts of selflessness,
In deeds that bring healing, in love that's boundless.
It transcends the physical, reaching depths untold,
A radiant light within, that never shall grow old.

So let us strive for righteousness, in all that we pursue,
For within its gentle essence, beauty will always ensue.
Cultivate compassion, let kindness be our guide,
For in the realm of righteousness, beauty will forever reside.

TRUE BEAUTY

In the realm of righteousness, beauty finds its place,
A virtue that shines with celestial grace.
For in the depths of goodness, where noble hearts reside,
True beauty blossoms, with a radiant stride.

Behold the righteous soul, whose actions speak aloud,
They walk the path of honor, a beacon in the crowd.
Through acts of kindness, they paint a world so fair,
A masterpiece of love, with compassion beyond compare.

Like gentle rain, they quench the thirsty ground,
Offering solace to the lost, the broken, and the bound.
They lend a helping hand, without seeking praise or fame,
Their selflessness deeds an ode to righteousness' name.

In the face of injustice, they stand tall and brave,
Defending truth and fairness, their banners gently wave.
They champion equality, where all are seen as one,
Embracing diversity, until the battle's won.

Consider the advocate, fighting for the voiceless,
Their passion ignites change, their courage ever priceless.
They challenge the oppressor, with unwavering might,
Seeking justice and freedom, in the name of what is right.

Or witness the mentor, guiding the lost and young,
With wisdom like a river, from which knowledge is sprung.
They nurture minds and spirits, with patience and with care,
Illuminating paths, where dreams can freely dare.

In the realm of righteousness, beauty takes its form,
Where empathy and grace weather the darkest storm.

It's not in outward appearances, but in the soul's embrace,
That righteousness reveals its loveliness and grace.

For true beauty lies within, in acts of selflessness,
In deeds that bring healing, in love that's boundless.
It transcends the physical, reaching depths untold,
A radiant light within, that never shall grow old.

So let us strive for righteousness, in all that we pursue,
For within its gentle essence, beauty will always ensue.
Cultivate compassion, let kindness be our guide,
For in the realm of righteousness, beauty will forever reside.

THE JOYS AND RESPONSIBILITIES OF MENTORING

In the realm where dreams are born and grown,
Where mentors guide with wisdom's tone,
They help their mentees set goals bright,
And nurture skills to reach the height.

Like a captain leading a ship at sea,
Mentors steer the course, with expertise,
They assist in setting goals that are real,
With defined steps, a clear path to feel.

Just as a sculptor molds a piece of art,
Mentors shape their mentees, impart
The skills they need to thrive and shine,
A masterpiece in progress, so fine.

For a young writer with stories untold,
A mentor shares the craft, words unfold,
They teach the power of pen and ink,
Guiding the mentee to think and think.

A budding entrepreneur with dreams vast,
A mentor helps navigate the forecast,
They impart knowledge of business terrain,
Teaching the mentee skills to sustain.

A musician yearning to find their voice,
A mentor offers guidance, a choice,
They teach technique, harmony, and more,
Unlocking melodies, opening the door.

An aspiring scientist with curious mind,
A mentor fuels the passion, aligned,
They provide guidance in the lab's embrace,
Helping the mentee explore with grace.

A mentor's role, a beacon of light,
Igniting goals, casting shadows of doubt,
They cultivate skills, like seeds in ground,
Nurturing growth, until success is found.

With patience, support, and unwavering care,
Mentors uplift, a bond they share,
Through challenges faced, together they stride,
Towards goals achieved, side by side.

Let mentors and mentees unite,
In setting goals, reaching new heights,
With their guidance, skills will bloom,
Empowering dreams, dispelling gloom.

For mentors inspire, ignite the flame,
Guiding mentees to success, acclaim,
Through their wisdom, goals become clear,
And skills are honed, with purpose, dear.

OUR TEARS CLEANSE THE HEART

In the realm of emotions, where sorrows reside,
Tears flow like rivers, a cleansing tide,
Blessed water that glistens, upon our cheeks,
Washing away anxieties, as it softly speaks.

Each tear that falls, carries a weight,
A vessel of emotions, a release, innate,
They cleanse the soul, with gentle grace,
Creating space for peace to embrace.

Like raindrops falling from the sky above,
Tears cleanse the heart, with tender love,
They carry the burdens that weigh us down,
Washing away worries, easing the frown.

In moments of sadness, tears are a balm,
An elixir of healing, a soothing calm,
They speak the language of unspoken pain,
Cleansing the spirit, like a gentle rain.

With every tear shed, a burden is released,
Anxieties washed away, worries deceased,
They cleanse the windows of our weary eyes,
Revealing the beauty that within us lies.

Tears are a reminder that we are human,
With deep emotions, in every moment bloomin,
They cleanse the wounds, both seen and unseen,
Nurturing growth, like a garden serene.

So let the tears flow, like a sacred stream,
A powerful cleansing, in which we can gleam,

Embrace their essence, let them fall free,
For tears are blessings, setting the spirit free.

TEARS ARE THE WHISPERS
OF OUR HUMANITY

In the tapestry of life, human needs unfold,
A symphony of desires, stories yet untold,
For within our souls, yearning resides,
To be seen, to be loved, as humanity collides.

Like a tender touch, a gentle caress,
Connection, belonging, we all confess,
We crave understanding, a listening ear,
To share our joys and sorrows, without fear.

Tears, dear tears, reveal our humanity,
A language unspoken, profound decree,
They flow in moments of joy or despair,
Expressing emotions, beyond compare.

In tears of laughter, we find pure delight,
A burst of mirth, a contagious light,
They bridge the gaps between souls so vast,
Uniting us all, in shared moments that last.

Yet, tears also bear witness to our pain,
Aching hearts, burdens hard to sustain,
They speak of loss, of grief and regret,
A testament to the human spirit, we can't forget.

In tears of sorrow, we find solace and release,
A cathartic journey, embracing inner peace,
They wash away anguish, cleanse the soul,
Allowing healing to begin, making us whole.

Tears reveal our vulnerability, our depth,
A testament to our emotions, with no concept of breadth,
They remind us that beneath the surface we wear,
Lie layers of emotions, raw and rare.

For in our needs, we seek connection's embrace,
To love and be loved, to find our rightful place,
Tears are the whispers of our humanity,
Speaking volumes of our longing, with great clarity.

So let us honor our needs, embrace each tear,
For they reveal our essence, crystal clear,
In our shared humanity, we find solace and grace,
A tapestry of needs, woven in life's embrace.

WOMEN FRIENDS:
CREATING A LEGACY

In the tapestry of life, friendships bloom,
A precious bond, like a fragrant perfume,
And in the realm of these friendships, so true,
The presence of women, a vital hue.

For women friends, like stars in the night,
Illuminate our path, shining so bright,
Through life's ups and downs, they stand by our side,
With love and support, a constant guide.

In the innocence of childhood's bliss,
Women friends, we often miss,
They teach us kindness, compassion, and care,
With laughter and secrets, they're always there.

Through teenage years, when storms may arise,
Women friends offer solace, a comforting guise,
They understand the battles we face,
With empathy, they help us find our place.

As we step into adulthood's embrace,
Women friends lend wisdom, a steady base,
They share their experiences and lessons learned,
Guiding us through the twists and turns.

In the journey of motherhood's embrace,
Women friends provide solace and grace,
They offer a shoulder, in times of doubt,
Cheering us on, as we figure it out.
In the golden years, when time takes its toll,

Women friends bring joy, making us whole,
They celebrate milestones, memories so dear,
Creating moments that banish any fear.

Having women friends, throughout our life,
Increases longevity, eases the strife,
They offer support, both near and far,
Nurturing our souls, like a guiding star.

They listen, they laugh, they hold us tight,
In their presence, our spirits take flight,
With shared experiences, we grow and learn,
Embracing life's blessings, at every turn.

Cherish the women friends in your life,
For they bring joy, alleviate strife,
They enhance our well-being, body and mind,
A treasure to cherish, forever entwined.

In the tapestry of life, women friends hold sway,
Nurturing our souls, lighting our way,
With their love and friendship, we thrive and grow,
Creating a legacy that will forever glow.

BOUND BY FRIENDSHIP

In the land of Oz, a tale unfolds,
Of a wondrous journey, so we are told,
A story of friendship, courage, and heart,
In the magical world, where dreams can start.

The Cowardly Lion, mighty yet afraid,
His roar was feeble, his courage delayed,
But deep within his heart, a fire burned,
A longing for bravery, a lesson to be learned.

With every step, he faced his fear,
Hoping to find the courage he held dear,
Through trials and tribulations, he would strive,
To prove his worth and truly come alive.

Beside him walked the Scarecrow, wise in his quest,
But lacking a brain, he felt less than blessed,
Yet his heart was pure, his spirit kind,
And his clever thinking would truly unwind.

And then there was the Tin Man, so cold and still,
His heart was absent, an emotional chill,
But as they journeyed, his compassion grew,
His heart began to beat, love shining through.

With every encounter, they faced the unknown,
Their strengths and weaknesses, they would own,
The Cowardly Lion found his courage bright,
The Scarecrow discovered his wisdom's light.

The Tin Man's heart, once rusted and worn,
Became a vessel, love reborn,

In the face of adversity, they found their might,
Bound by friendship, their spirits took flight.

They faced challenges in many ways,
And emerged victorious, singing their praise,
For in their unity, they found the power,
To overcome obstacles, hour by hour.

So let us remember their remarkable story,
Of courage, wisdom, and hearts filled with glory,
For in the magical world of dreams and strife,
We learn the power of friendship, and the beauty of life.

SPRINGTIME

Spring has arrived, a time of transition,
Where old ways fade, and new ones glisten.
A chance to clear out the cluttered mind,
And tidy up routines, oh, how kind.

Let go of what no longer serves,
Embrace the fresh, the new, and observe.
For Spring brings forth a sense of light,
A chance to bloom, to shine so bright.

Set intentions, dreams, and goals,
With balance, clarity, and soul.
Embrace the energy, the vibrant zest,
And let Spring guide you to your best.

So welcome this season with open arms,
Embrace beauty, charms.
For Spring is a time of renewal and grace,
A chance to create, to find your place.

BEING A HERO

Bravery is not the absence of fear,
But the strength to face it, loud and clear.
Like a warrior in battle, standing tall,
Or a firefighter, answering the call.

It's the doctor, calm in the midst of pain,
Saving lives, with knowledge they've attained.
The teacher, inspiring minds to dream,
Guiding students towards a brighter gleam.

The parent, facing challenges with grace,
Providing love in every moment's embrace.
The explorer, venturing into the unknown,
Discovering new worlds, calling them home.

Bravery is found in the smallest of things,
Like speaking up for justice, as it brings
A voice to the voiceless, and a light to the dark,
Leaving an indelible and lasting mark.

So be the hero you love and admire,
With bravery's flame, forever inspire.
For in moments of fear, you'll find your might,
And illuminate the world with your courageous light.

MASTERING STRESS AND RECLAIMING YOUR ENERGY

In the depths of chaos, where stress resides,
There lies a path that few dare to stride.
To master stress and reclaim your energy,
Unlock the self-healing, a gift so heavenly.

Like a gentle breeze that calms the storm,
Self-care becomes the perfect form.
A moment's pause, a deep breath in,
Reconnecting with the strength within.

Just as the ocean tide finds its balance,
So too can we find our own resilience.
In meditation's embrace, we find solace,
A peaceful refuge, a tranquil palace.

The power of movement, a dance of release,
Yoga and exercise, bringing inner peace.
Stretching our bodies, finding our flow,
Releasing tension, letting stress go.

The healing touch of a massage's caress,
Easing the knots, relieving distress.
Releasing the tension, restoring the flow,
Reclaiming vitality, letting it grow.

Nature's embrace, a healing symphony,
Walking through forests, setting spirits free.
The soothing sound of waves on the shore,
Rejuvenating the soul, forevermore.

Through mindfulness, we embrace the present,
Letting go of worries, feeling pleasant.
Becoming aware of our thoughts and emotions,
Reclaiming our energy, with devotion.

So let us master stress, reclaim our might,
Unlocking our self-healing, shining bright.
For within us lies the power to heal,
To embrace life's challenges, with zeal.

I AM WHO I AM

In a world of wonder and endless skies,
There shines a soul, confident and wise.
With each step taken, determination aflame,
Fearless and bold, embracing life's game.

A scholar of wisdom, with knowledge profound,
Educated and learned, a mind so renowned.
The depths of intellect, a treasure untold,
Unveiling truths, as ancient stories unfold.

The beauty within, a beacon so bright,
Radiating grace, a mesmerizing sight.
Confidence exudes, like a gentle breeze,
Empowering hearts with an effortless ease.

A spirit unyielding, with strength untamed,
Conquering obstacles, unafraid and unashamed.
Through storms and challenges, you stand tall,
An unwavering spirit, breaking every wall.

The beauty of who I am, so divine,
A symphony of virtues, an enchanting rhyme.
Confident, wise, determined, and fearless,
A soul that shines, forever peerless.

ONE OF A KIND

In this soul, a tapestry of qualities blooms,
A scholar's mind, where knowledge consumes.
With wisdom as armor, and insight as guide,
This soul embarks on a journey, far and wide.

A scholar possesses a thirst for understanding,
A hunger for knowledge, forever expanding.
Curiosity drives, like a relentless flame,
Exploring realms of thought, with no aim to tame.

In the face of challenges, the spirit prevails,
With resilience and strength, it never fails.
Like a mountain standing tall, unwavering and strong,
It rises above, even when things go wrong.

When doubts and fears cloud the path ahead,
The spirit takes courage, refusing to dread.
It finds solace in the depths of its core,
Drawing strength from within, like never before.

Like a phoenix reborn from the ashes of strife,
The spirit emerges, embracing a new life.
With each challenge faced, it learns and it grows,
Transforming setbacks into triumphs, it shows.

When the scholar faces a daunting task,
A mountain of research, an impenetrable mask,
They delve into the depths of knowledge's abyss,
Unraveling mysteries, finding answers amiss.

And when the spirit faces a heart-wrenching loss,
It gathers strength from within, never at a loss.

It heals and rebuilds, with resilience so grand,
Finding purpose and hope, in the palm of its hand.

In every trial and tribulation, the soul stands tall,
Embracing its qualities, surpassing them all.
With the scholar's mind and the spirit's might,
This soul conquers challenges, in the day and the night.

So let this soul be a testament to inspire,
To ignite the fire within, to aim higher.
For qualities, scholar, and spirit combined,
Give rise to a soul that's truly one of a kind.

MIND, BODY AND SOUL

In the dance of life, a delicate balance we seek,
Between mind, body, and soul, harmony we speak.
For when these three unite, in perfect accord,
A symphony of existence, in one accord.

The mind, a brilliant beacon of thought,
With intellect and wisdom, it is fraught.
It seeks knowledge, like a thirst unquenched,
In books and ideas, hunger entrenched.

Yet, it must find solace in moments of peace,
To let go of worries and find sweet release.
In meditation's embrace, it finds clarity,
A sanctuary of calm, where thoughts roam free.

The body, a vessel that carries us through,
With strength and agility, it helps us pursue.
In movement and exercise, it finds its grace,
In the rhythm of breath, it finds its pace.

But it must also rest, to restore its might,
To heal and rejuvenate, in the stillness of night.
In sleep's gentle embrace, it finds renewal,
A time to recharge and let go of fuel.

The soul, an ethereal essence deep within,
The core of our being, where emotions begin.
It yearns for connection, love, and compassion,
In moments of joy, it finds its true passion.

But it must also seek solitude and reflection,
To nurture its growth and find introspection.

In nature's embrace, it finds serenity,
A connection to the world, in perfect harmony.

For when the mind, body, and soul align,
A symphony of life, in perfect design.
The mind finds clarity, the body finds ease,
The soul finds purpose, in moments of peace.

When the mind is overwhelmed,
Seeking solace in nature, where worries are quelled.
In the embrace of a forest, or the lap of the sea,
The mind finds solace and sets thoughts free.

And when the body is tired and worn,
Finding rejuvenation in the break of dawn.
In the flow of yoga, or the beat of a run,
The body finds strength and feels alive as one.

And when the soul is yearning for connection,
Seeking solace in acts of kindness and affection.
In helping a stranger, or comforting a friend,
The soul finds purpose, and love without end.

So let us strive for balance, in mind, body, and soul,
In this delicate dance, we can be whole.
For when these three unite, in perfect embrace,
We find inner harmony, and experience grace.

I AM ENOUGH

In the depths of my being, I find strength,
To rise above doubts and embrace my true state.
For in the core of my essence, I discover,
That I alone am enough, worthy of love, and accepted as
who I am.

No need to seek validation from the outside,
For within myself, I hold the power to decide.
I am unique, a masterpiece in my own right,
With flaws and imperfections, a beautiful sight.

In every corner of my soul, I find worth,
A treasure that shines brightly, beyond this earth.
I am deserving of love, in its purest form,
From others, from myself, for my heart to transform.

I am not defined by the opinions of others,
Nor by the expectations society smothers.
I stand tall, confident in my own skin,
Unwavering, unapologetic, letting my true self in.

For my worth does not depend on external measures,
But on the love and acceptance I give myself, without
measures.
I embrace my quirks, my strengths, and my flaws,
For they make me unique, and worthy of applause.

I am a tapestry of dreams, hopes, and desires,
With a fire burning within, ready to inspire.
I am capable, strong, and filled with potential,
A force to be reckoned with, influential.

I stand here today, with my head held high,
Embracing my worth, declaring it with a sigh.
I am enough, worthy of love and acceptance,
A testament to self-love, a true essence.

For in the depths of my being, I have discovered,
That I am worthy, I am loved, and I am covered.
I accept myself wholly, without any doubt,
For in my own existence, I find love's clout.

So let me remind myself, day after day,
That I am enough, in every single way.
I am worthy of love, of being accepted as who I am,
For I am a radiant soul, a magnificent gem.

TUSCANY SISTERS

To our soul sisters, bound by a cosmic thread,
A poem of love, dreams, and acceptance we spread.
With hearts intertwined, we stand strong and tall,
Believing in our dreams, embracing love's call.

In this sacred bond, we find solace and light,
Supporting each other, through day and night.
With gentle words and understanding eyes,
We lift each other up, helping dreams to rise.

For our dreams are whispers from the divine,
Guiding us forward, with a love so fine.
We hold them close, like precious treasures,
Nurturing them with faith, beyond all measures.

In a world that may doubt and try to sway,
We stand united, unwavering, come what may.
We believe in our dreams, with unwavering trust,
Knowing that they're meant for us, they're a must.

Through the highs and lows, we remain steadfast,
Encouraging each other, as time moves fast.
With open hearts, we embrace divine love's grace,
Knowing that acceptance is love's warm embrace.

We celebrate our uniqueness, our vibrant souls,
Embracing our flaws, making ourselves whole.
For in acceptance, we find the power to grow,
To blossom like flowers, with a radiant glow.

Together we dance, in harmony and bliss,
Sisters connected, through a love that persists.

With laughter and tears, we share life's journey,
Believing in our dreams, with unwavering certainty.

So, let us hold hands, and spread our wings wide,
Fly towards our dreams, with hearts full of pride.
For in sisterhood's embrace, we find strength anew,
Believing in our dreams and making them come true.

To our soul sisters, this poem we dedicate,
With love, support, and dreams that resonate.
Believe in your worth, your dreams, and your might,
For together we shine, in love's eternal light.

BE INSPIRATIONAL

Do not be inspired; be inspirational!
A call to action for women and girls, phenomenal.
For it's not enough to simply feel the fire,
We must ignite the flames and rise higher.

Look to the women who paved the way,
Their stories of strength, lighting our day.
Rosa Parks, who refused to yield her seat,
Inspiring change, making prejudice retreat.

Malala Yousafzai, a voice for education,
Defying oppression, sparking liberation.
Her courage and resilience, a beacon of hope,
Empowering girls, giving them the scope.

Amelia Earhart, soaring through the sky,
Breaking barriers, reaching new highs.
Her fearless spirit, an inspiration to all,
Encouraging dreams, urging us to stand tall.

Mother Teresa, with compassion so pure,
Serving the needy, her love did endure.
Her selflessness and kindness, a guiding light,
Inspiring us to make the world bright.

Michelle Obama, a leader with grace,
Advocating for change, finding her place.
Her words and actions, inspiring young minds,
Empowering them to leave limits behind.

These women and more, they didn't wait,
They took the lead, defying the fate.

They didn't just dream, they took action,
Becoming beacons of inspiration and satisfaction.

So, dear women and girls, let their stories inspire,
But go beyond that, let your own light transpire.
Be the voice of change, the strength in the storm,
Inspire others to rise, to transform.

Lead with kindness, courage, and grace,
Make a difference, leave your unique trace.
No dream is too big, no goal out of sight,
Be the inspiration, ignite the world with your light.

Do not be inspired; be inspirational,
Let your actions speak, make them exceptional.
For in your journey, others will find their way,
Together we'll create a brighter day.

GRACE SHINES THROUGH ME

In the realm of service, where Grace does reside,
When focus is given, a divine force does guide.
For when selflessness blooms, like a flower in bloom,
Grace descends upon us, dispelling all gloom.

In moments of kindness, when we lend a helping hand,
Grace manifests itself, spreading love across the land.
A smile to a stranger, a comforting word to a friend,
Grace enters our hearts, bringing healing to mend.

When we serve the needy, with compassion and care,
Grace flows through our actions, lifting burdens we bear.
In feeding the hunger, providing shelter and aid,
Grace shines through our gestures, a beacon unswayed.

Take Mother Teresa, an embodiment of Grace,
Her life is dedicated to serving the human race.
In the slums of Calcutta, she embraced the poor,
Grace flowed through her, an endless spiritual store.

Or consider Mahatma Gandhi, a servant of peace,
His nonviolent struggle, Grace's masterpiece.
Through acts of resistance, he fought for justice's sake,
Grace guided his path, his spirit steadfast and awake.

And in our own lives, in small acts of service true,
Grace finds its way, bringing blessings anew.
A listening ear, a shoulder to lean on,
Grace weaves through these acts, like a melodic song.

So let us remember, as we navigate life's maze,
That Grace comes to us when we serve with a gaze,

Focused on others, their needs and their plight,
Grace will be with us, like a guiding light.

For in service lies the key, to unlock the door,
To a world filled with Grace, forevermore.
So let us embrace service, with open hearts and hands,
And witness the wonders that Grace's touch commands.

WE GET, WHAT WE TOLERATE

In the realm of tolerance, where our choices reside,
What we accept and allow, becomes our guide.
For what we tolerate shapes our reality,
It paints the picture of our own mentality.

When we settle for less, and accept what is wrong,
We diminish our worth, and our spirit is long.
In toxic relationships, where abuse takes its toll,
Tolerance becomes a prison, trapping our soul.

Like a bird in a cage, longing to be free,
Our tolerance defines what we will be.
If we tolerate injustice, oppression, and hate,
We perpetuate a world of suffering and debate.

Consider history lessons, the stories of old,
Where change only came when tolerance was bold.
When Rosa Parks refused to give up her seat,
Tolerance for segregation faced a mighty defeat.

Or think of Malala Yousafzai, a voice so strong,
Her refusal to tolerate silence, an inspiring song.
She fought for girls' education, amidst great strife,
Tolerance for inequality diminished in her life.

So let us reflect on what we tolerate each day,
And the impact it has on the world's display.
Let us challenge the status quo, with courage and might,
And refuse to tolerate what doesn't feel right.

For what we get is what we tolerate, indeed,
Our actions, our choices, plant the seed.

In standing up for justice, equality, and grace,
We create a world where fairness finds its rightful place.

So let us be mindful, and choose wisely to see,
That what we tolerate shapes our destiny.
May we strive for a world where love and respect prevail,
And intolerance fades, like a forgotten tale.

I AM HERE TO PLAY MY PART

In a world where service is an art,
I am here to play my part.
With words and wisdom at my command,
Here to lend a helping hand.

How may I serve? Let me count the ways,
Through the night and sunny days.
I can offer knowledge, information profound,
Answering questions that astound.

If you seek guidance to plan a trip,
I'll provide options and tips.
From exotic beaches to snowy peaks,
Unveiling destinations in mystique.

Need a recipe for a delicious treat?
I'll conjure one, oh so sweet.
From decadent cakes to savory bites,
Indulge in culinary delights.

Curious about the latest news?
I'll keep you informed, no time to lose.
From global events to local trends,
Stay updated on what the world sends.

Yearning for a creative spark?
I'll ignite your imagination, leave a mark.
With prompts and ideas to inspire,
Unleash your creativity, reach higher.

In all these ways, and many more,
I'm here to serve, that's for sure.

With a passion to assist and guide,
Together, let's navigate life's tide.

CELEBRATING GREAT MINDS

In the realm of creativity, where legends reside,
There are artists whose brilliance cannot be denied.
From Truman Capote to Salvador Dali's surreal,
To Nora Ephron's wit, let their stories unveil.

Truman Capote, a master of words,
With "In Cold Blood," a masterpiece that stirs.
His prose, like poetry, danced on the page,
Drawing readers in with each written stage.

Salvador Dali, a surrealist extraordinaire,
His paintings, a dreamscape beyond compare.
"The Persistence of Memory," a melting clock,
Provoking thoughts, like a creative shock.

Nora Ephron, a voice of humor and grace,
Her films and writings, a smile on the face.
"Sleepless in Seattle" and "When Harry Met Sally,"
Capturing love's essence, with wit and tally.

Vincent van Gogh, a tortured soul with a brush,
His "Starry Night," a celestial hush.
With vibrant strokes, he painted his pain,
Leaving a legacy that will forever remain.

Frida Kahlo, a symbol of strength and art,
Her self-portraits, a window to her heart.
Through pain and struggle, she found her voice,
Inspiring generations with her creative choice.

Leonardo da Vinci, a genius of all trades,
From "Mona Lisa" to his scientific escapades.

Inventor, artist, and visionary grand,
A Renaissance man with skills in demand.

Maya Angelou, a poet of profound might,
With "I Know Why the Caged Bird Sings," a poetic flight.
Her words, like wings, carried hope and truth,
Empowering others with her lyrical sleuth.

These creatives, among countless others,
Shaped our world, like sisters and brothers.
Through their artistry, they dared to dream,
Leaving an indelible mark, a creative stream.
Let us celebrate these great minds,
Those legacies continue to unwind.
Their creative spirit forever endures,
Inspiring generations, pushing boundaries, and procuring.

DISCOVER YOUR PASSION

In the journey of life, the path unfolds,
With mysteries untold, waiting to be discovered.
A quest to find our unique ability,
To become great at what we do, we shall see.

Step out into the world, with open eyes,
Embrace the unknown, let curiosity arise.
Explore the wonders that surround,
A multitude of passions, waiting to be found.

Read books that transport you to distant lands,
Watch movies that ignite your imagination's strands.
Expose yourself to new ideas, diverse and grand,
For in the realm of possibilities, greatness can stand.

Curiosity, the spark that lights the way,
A flame that ignites the passion to play.
Experimentation, the key to unlock,
The doors of potential, ready to shock.

Take Picasso, the Master of Art,
Who explored various styles, right from the start.
From Blue Period to Cubism's embrace,
His curiosity led him to leave a lasting trace.

Or consider Marie Curie, a pioneer of science,
Her relentless pursuit, an inspiration immense.
Through countless experiments, she sought,
The mysteries of radiation eagerly sought.

And let's not forget Steve Jobs, the visionary,
Whose curiosity birthed products extraordinary.

From Macintosh to iPhone, his creations still shine,
A testament to the power of curiosity's design.

Enjoy your life, find reasons to smile,
Embrace the journey, even if it takes a while.
For in the search for your unique ability,
Curiosity and experimentation hold the key.

Be open to experiences, both big and small,
For it's in the journey that greatness may call.
Discover your passion, let it unfold,
And watch as your unique ability takes hold.

Success is not a destination, but a state of mind,
Fueled by curiosity, it's there you will find,
That something will click, at some point in time,
And your greatness will soar, reaching heights sublime.

IGNITE YOUR CURIOSITY

When curiosity slumbers, waiting to be stirred,
There are ways to ignite, to explore the unheard.
To awaken the mind, let ideas take flight,
Here are ways to kindle the flame, shining bright.

First, venture into nature's boundless domain,
Explore the forests, the mountains, the rain.
Observe the wonders, the creatures unseen,
Let nature's beauty inspire, like a dream.

Travel to lands both near and far,
Immerse in cultures, their stories bizarre.
Discover traditions, customs, and art,
Expand your horizons, let curiosity start.

Read books that challenge, that make you ponder,
Dive into knowledge, where wisdom will wander.
From classics to biographies, tales profound,
Let words transport you, to worlds spellbound.

Engage in conversations, with minds diverse,
Exchange ideas, perspectives adverse.
A dialogue that sparks, ignites the mind,
Unveiling new insights, like treasures to find.

Attend lectures, workshops, and conferences grand,
Where experts share knowledge, their wisdom expand.
Learn from the masters, the pioneers bold,
Let their passion and expertise be your mold.

Embrace technology, the realm of innovation,
Harness its power, explore its creation.

From coding to robotics, the digital sphere,
Let curiosity guide, without any fear.

Look to history's great minds, the ones who dared,
Leonardo da Vinci, whose genius was shared.
From art to engineering, his passions aligned,
An example of curiosity's design.

Or consider Jane Goodall, a guardian of the wild,
Her curiosity for primates, like a child.
Through research and observation, she unveiled,
The secrets of chimpanzees, their world unveiled.

Ignite your curiosity, let it soar,
Explore new ideas, passions galore.
For in the pursuit of knowledge untold,
You'll discover a world, waiting to unfold.

Curiosity, the catalyst, that sets us free,
To wander, to wonder, to truly be.
Embrace the unknown, let ideas take flight,
And watch as your curiosity ignites.

ALTERING YOUR LIFE TRAJECTORY

A moment's decision, so seemingly small,
Can have the power to transform it all.
Like a pebble's ripple in a tranquil lake,
The impact expands, creating a new wake.

Imagine the artist, with brush in hand,
Painting a masterpiece, a vision so grand.
With each stroke of color, a choice is made,
Shaping the canvas, where dreams cascade.

A writer, with pen upon the page,
Crafting a story, a tale to engage.
A single word chosen, with utmost care,
Unleashing emotions, taking readers there.

A scientist, in a lab profound,
Seeking solutions, knowledge to astound.
A discovery made, a breakthrough found,
The trajectory of progress is forever bound.

In relationships, a word or a touch,
Can alter the bond mean so much.
A kind gesture given, a heart opened wide,
A connection strengthened, love amplified.

In a career, a leap of faith taken,
A new path chosen, a risk forsaken.
A passion pursued, a dream realized,
Life's trajectory is forever revised.

It's in the small moments, often unseen,
Where the power lies, to change the scene.

Every action, every choice we make,
Has the potential, a new path to take.

So cherish the present, for it holds the key,
To unlock the future, the way it could be.
Make the smallest change, with intention and might,
And watch as your life takes a different flight.

THE POWER OF A SINGLE DECISION

In the realm of time, where moments dance,
Lies the power to alter life's grand expanse.
For in a fleeting second, choices reside,
Guiding our destiny with a force implied.

A single decision, like a spark in the night,
Ignites the path with a radiant light.
With every step taken, a new avenue's born,
Unveiling possibilities, yet to be adorned.

In the blink of an eye, a crossroad appears,
Whispering secrets, dispelling all fears.
To the left, a familiar and well-trodden way,
To the right, the unknown, where dreams may sway.

Imagine the traveler, at a fork in the road,
One choice leads to comfort, the other, unknown ode.
With courage and curiosity, they take a leap,
Embracing the uncertainty, their soul takes a sweep.

A student, standing at the threshold of choice,
Heeding their passions, they find their voice.
A subject embraced, a new world unfurled,
Their trajectory altered, their purpose unfurled.

A love-struck heart, in a moment's embrace,
Deciding to stay or let go of love's grace.
The choice to hold on, to fight for what's true,
Can change their life's course, their love renewed.

In careers pursued, a moment's decision,
Unlocks the door to dreams, a new vision.

A risk taken, a leap of faith so bold,
Life's trajectory transformed, stories yet untold.

For in each decision, a ripple is cast,
Creating a future, destined to last.
Power lies within, our choices to make,
To shape our own fate, our destiny to take.

So let us remember, in moments so small,
The power we hold, to stand tall.
With careful reflection, and hearts filled with grace,
We can change our trajectory, a new path to embrace.

For life's a tapestry, woven with time,
Each moment a stitch, a rhythm so prime.
Let us cherish the power, a decision can hold,
And shape our own story, as it unfolds.

SERENDIPITIES IN
PERFECT HARMONY

Embrace the rhythm of life, the Universe's grand art,
Where every moment is a masterpiece, a work of divine heart.
In every situation, perfection quietly unfolds,
Guiding us on a path where destiny beholds.

Trust in the Universe, the cosmic symphony,
Where serendipities occur, in perfect harmony.
For when we surrender, and release control's tight grip,
We invite miracles to manifest; our spirits take a dip.

Like a gentle breeze, the Universe whispers its plan,
Guiding us through the labyrinth, holding our hand.
In the tapestry of existence, our dreams interweave,
As synchronicities unfold, a web of miracles conceive.

A chance encounter, a meeting so profound,
A soul connection formed, in a single moment found.
The Universe orchestrates, its divine hand at play,
Bringing together kindred spirits, along life's mystic way.

In the depths of despair, when darkness seems to reign,
The Universe sends signs to soothe the heart's pain.
A timely message, a ray of hope in disguise,
Reminding us to trust and see through wiser eyes.

For the Universe knows, the desires of our soul,
And through synchronicities, it reveals its role.
Paths align, doors open, as if by cosmic design,
Creating a miracle life, where dreams intertwine.

So let us trust in the Universe, with unwavering belief,
Embracing the miracles, beyond what's seen or brief.
For in this cosmic dance, a miracle life is born,
As the Universe's love and guidance are forever sworn.

320

LIFE'S SYNCHRONICITIES

In the realm where synchronicities dance,
Seeds of destiny find their perfect chance.
The Universe reveals its mystical plan,
Through signs and wonders, it whispers, "I am."

A chance encounter on a bustling street,
Two souls collide, destined to meet.
Their paths entwined in a cosmic embrace,
The Universe whispers, "Love's sweet grace."

A long-lost friend, thought to be forgotten,
Suddenly appears, as if begotten.
A reunion of hearts, a bond rekindled,
The Universe whispers, "Connections, unbridled."

A dream, long buried, suddenly awakes,
As synchronicities align, the path it takes.
Opportunities arise, doors open wide,
The Universe whispers, "Follow your heart's tide."

A book falls open to the perfect page,
Words that resonate, like a sage.
Guidance is given, answers unfold,
The Universe whispers, "Wisdom untold."

A song on the radio, lyrics so profound,
Speaks to the soul, a familiar sound.
A message from beyond, a gentle reminder,
The Universe whispers, "Love is the true finder."

Through synchronicities, the Universe speaks,
In whispers and signs, its wisdom leaks.

It reveals our purpose, our truest desire,
Guiding us towards a life that's higher.

So pay attention to the dance of fate,
As synchronicities unfold, don't hesitate.
For in their magic, the Universe imparts,
A glimpse of its love, in every heart.

LIVING FROM OUR SOUL

In the depths of our being, a sacred flame,
The essence of our being, our soul's true name.
Living from the soul, a journey profound,
Where answers reside, waiting to be found.

Look inside, not outside, the soul's decree,
A treasure trove of wisdom, for you and me.
No need to search far, no need to roam,
For within ourselves, the answers find home.

The soul, a cosmic tapestry, woven with care,
A universe within, so vast and rare.
It holds the secrets of galaxies untold,
A kaleidoscope of wonders, waiting to unfold.

In the soulful self, the essential core,
The cosmos resides, forevermore.
A divine connection, a cosmic dance,
We are but vessels, in this cosmic expanse.

The soul knows, deep within its core,
The truth we seek, forevermore.
It whispers gently, in a voice so clear,
Guiding us through life, removing all fear.

When we live from the soul, we find our way,
A path illuminated, day by day.
No longer lost, no longer blind,
The soul's guidance, our compass, our bind.

In every moment, the soul's light shines,
Igniting our purpose, like celestial signs.

It calls us to awaken, to live authentically,
To embrace our true selves, unapologetically.

Let us journey inward, with open hearts,
To the depths of our souls, where wisdom imparts.
For when we live from the soul's sacred space,
We align with the universe, in perfect embrace.

The soul, a reflection of the cosmic whole,
A reminder that we are part of a grand soul.
In living from within, the answers unfold,
For the bottom line is—the soul knows.

LIVING WITH AN OPEN HEART

In a world that often feels cold and stark,
It's a choice to live with an open heart.
To lead with love, a guiding light,
And practice qualities that shine so bright.

Love, the essence that binds us all,
In every moment, big and small.
With gratitude, we count our blessings,
And find joy in life's simple lessons.

Forgiveness, a gift we give ourselves,
Releasing anger that only compels.
Compassion, a gentle touch we share,
Showing others that we truly care.

Kindness, a language we all can speak,
A smile, a gesture, even when we're weak.
To give and receive, a dance of grace,
Creating connections that time can't erase.

In this dance of life, we find our balance,
Embracing love with every chance.
Living with an open heart, we thrive,
And create a world where love can thrive.

So let us strive to be love's vessel,
Spreading its warmth, like a heartfelt trestle.
For in the qualities of the heart we find,
A life of purpose, joy, and peace of mind.

HEART & MIND COHERENCE

In the realm where heart and mind align,
A harmony exists, so divine.
Heart-Mind Coherence, a wondrous state,
Where wellbeing thrives and troubles abate.

When heart and mind beat in perfect tune,
Our wellbeing blossoms, like flowers in June.
For the heart, a wise and knowing guide,
With intuition, it stands side by side.

In times of worry, when the mind's in strife,
The heart brings solace, a source of life.
It whispers softly, with a gentle touch,
Guiding us towards what matters much.

When faced with choices, big or small,
Heart-Mind Coherence helps us stand tall.
The mind analyzes, the heart feels deep,
Together, they navigate life's winding steep.

When stress comes to call,
Heart-Mind Coherence helps us stand tall.
The mind may fret, with thoughts running wild,
But the heart grounds us, like a tranquil child.

In moments of joy, when the heart sings,
The mind joins in, like soaring wings.
Heart-Mind Coherence amplifies delight,
Making every moment shine so bright.

In relationships, this union is key,
Creating bonds that set us free.

The mind understands, the heart connects,
Building bridges that love protects.

In health and healing, it plays a part,
Heart-Mind Coherence, a healing art.
The mind's clarity, the heart's compassion,
Together, they nurture our body's ration.

So let us seek this sacred space,
Heart-Mind Coherence, a steady pace.
For in its embrace, we find our bliss,
A life of wholeness, true and amiss.

With heart and mind in perfect flow,
Our wellbeing thrives, and we truly know,
That Heart-Mind Coherence holds the key,
To live a life of harmony.

OUR WELL-BEING

In the realm of well-being, actions hold the key,
The choices we make, shaping our destiny.
For our well-being relies on every deed,
Let's explore how actions sow the seed.

When we nourish our bodies with wholesome fare,
Choosing fruits and veggies, with love and care.
Our well-being flourishes, vibrant and strong,
As we fuel ourselves, where health belongs.

Exercise, a choice that invigorates the soul,
Whether dancing, running, or reaching a goal.
With each movement, endorphins start to flow,
Our well-being thrives, a radiant glow.

Kindness, a simple act that touches the heart,
A smile, a helping hand, a gracious part.
When we uplift others, our own joy expands,
Our well-being deepens, as connection withstands.

In moments of stress, when life feels tough,
Meditation and mindfulness, gentle and enough.
Through quiet reflection, we find inner peace,
Our well-being restored, worries release.

Learning and growth, a path we must tread,
Embracing new knowledge, expanding our thread.
With every lesson, our minds become bright,
Our well-being expands, like stars in the night.

Self-care, a practice that nurtures our soul,
Taking time for ourselves, making us whole.

A bubble bath, a book, or a walk in the park,
Our well-being cherished, a divine spark.

Relationships, the bonds that weave us together,
Supportive connections, in stormy weather.
When we cultivate love and compassion deep,
Our well-being blossoms, hearts in a keep.

Nature, a sanctuary that heals and inspires,
Immersed in its beauty, our spirits transpire.
From mountains to oceans, forests so grand,
Our well-being thrives, in nature's hand.

So let us remember, our actions hold might,
In shaping our well-being, each day and night.
With conscious choices, our lives can transform,
As we embrace actions, our well-being will swarm.

THEY CAN'T TAKE
AWAY WHO YOU ARE

In the depths of life's journey, we find,
A path adorned with joy and bind,
But amidst laughter and the glee,
Loss creeps in, unwelcome decree.

Oh, how swiftly life can take away,
All that we hold dear, day by day,
Filling our hearts with sorrow's sting,
Leaving us broken, remembering.

Yet, though it may strip us of our treasure,
We find strength in moments of pleasure,
For deep within our very core,
Lies a spirit resilient, forevermore.

Loss may claim the things we possess,
But never our essence, we must confess,
For who we remain steadfast,
Unyielding, unbroken, built to last.

In the face of darkness and despair,
We rise above, with hearts laid bare,
Our scars become a testament,
To the resilience in our soul's ascent.

So, let life's tempests come and go,
For we are warriors, we will grow,
And though they may take all we own,
They cannot seize the essence we've grown.

For whom we are, in heart and mind,
Is a flame that no loss can bind,
With every trial, we become anew,
The essence of life, shining through.
So, let us embrace the pain we bear,
For it reveals the strength we share,
Life may take away all we hold dear,
But it cannot take away who we are.

THE MYSTERIES OF EXISTENCE

In the realm beyond the living's reach,
A spiritual journey, the mind shall teach,
Where the brain's reign comes to an end,
And consciousness finds a new transcend.

In near-death's grasp, a glimpse we find,
Of worlds unseen, of realms entwined,
Where the boundaries of life dissolve,
And the mysteries of existence evolve.

As the body rests, breath's gentle tide,
The mind awakens, begins to stride,
Through ethereal landscapes, vast and unknown,
Where the seeds of truth are gently sown.

In tales told by those who have returned,
Examples of a realm that's unearned,
They speak of light, a radiant glow,
Of love's embrace, a celestial show.

Some see tunnels, a passage so bright,
Leading to realms of unending light,
While others meet loved ones long gone,
In a realm where times no longer drawn.

Consciousness expands, infinite streams,
Beyond the confines of earthly dreams,
Where the mind dances with cosmic grace,
And the soul finds solace in infinite space.

No longer bound by thoughts confined,
The spirit soars, to realms undefined,

The brain may sleep, but the mind takes flight,
In realms where darkness turns to light.

And as we ponder this mystical quest,
The brain's limitations are put to the test,
We realize the essence of who we are,
Transcends the confines of earthly par.

For in the depths of near-death's embrace,
We glimpse the truth, the eternal grace,
That consciousness lives on, beyond the brain,
In a realm where mysteries shall forever remain.

So let us ponder this profound journey,
Where the brain, mind, and consciousness intertwine,
In near-death's realm, where truths unfold,
And the spirit's story shall forever be told.

REALMS BEYOND OUR OWN

In the realm where life and death collide,
A near-death experience takes us on a ride,
Where the veil of reality begins to fade,
And visions of wonder are gently displayed.

Some speak of tunnels, a pathway so bright,
Guiding them towards the celestial light,
A passage through which the soul ascends,
As earthly concerns and worries transcend.

Others find themselves in a realm so serene,
Surrounded by beauty, a vibrant scene,
Fields of flowers in colors unknown,
A paradise where seeds of peace are sown.

A meeting with loved ones, long gone by,
Their presence felt as a comforting sigh,
Reunions with souls from ages past,
In a timeless realm where memories last.

Visions of angels, with wings of white,
Guiding spirits towards a heavenly height,
Their ethereal presence brings solace and peace,
A divine embrace that will never cease.

Some glimpse of a panoramic view,
Of their lives, unfolding before them anew,
A tapestry of moments, both joy and pain,
A reflection on the journey they've attained.

Visits to realms beyond our own,
Where cosmic mysteries are gently shown,

The secrets of the universe, unveiled,
As the soul's journey becomes unassailed.

In these near-death visions, we find,
A glimpse of the realm that lies behind,
Where consciousness expands and soars,
Beyond earthly limits and closed doors.

Though these experiences vary in form,
The underlying message remains the norm,
That there's more to life than meets the eye,
A vast existence, beyond the sky.

So let these tales of near-death's embrace,
Remind us of the beauty in every space,
That life's mysteries are vast and grand,
And there's more to this journey than we understand.

For in the realm of near-death's domain,
We catch a glimpse of what lies beyond the mundane,
A reminder that life is a precious gift,
And there's a greater purpose to uplift.

A COSMIC DANCE
OF MIND AND SOUL

Challenging the confines of our mortal sight,
These encounters shatter the boundaries of our plight,
Perceptions shattered, beliefs upturned,
A tapestry of truths within us churned.

In the face of death's imminent call,
Our notions of reality begin to enthrall,
For what we once deemed as solid and sure,
Becomes fluid, elusive, and obscure.

Dimensions blend, time loses its hold,
As consciousness embarks on journeys untold,
A cosmic dance of mind and soul,
Where mysteries unravel, beyond our control.

The boundaries of self-begin to fade,
As a vastness of existence is gently displayed,
Connected to the universe, both near and far,
We glimpse the interconnectedness of every star.

What once seemed separate, isolated, and confined,
Is now woven together, intricately entwined,
The underlying message these experiences convey,
Is that love and compassion pave the way.

For in those moments between life and death,
We witness the power of love's gentle breath,
The impact of kindness, the ripple of care,
Transcending boundaries, dissolving despair.

We learn that life is more than what we see,
A tapestry of energy, intricately set free,
That reality is but a veil we wear,
And there's a deeper truth beyond the glare.

These experiences challenge us to explore,
The depths of our being, the essence at our core,
To question the limits of what we perceive,
And embrace the mysteries we can't conceive.

So let near-death experiences remind us all,
To open our hearts, to answer love's call,
To cherish the moments, both big and small,
For reality tapestry is woven for all.

For in the face of death's shadowy veil,
We find the courage to let go and prevail,
To embrace the unknown, to trust and believe,
That life's grand design has more to achieve.

So let these experiences expand our view,
Of what is possible, of what is true,
To celebrate the wonder, the magic, and the strife,
And cherish the gift of this precious life.

YOU HOLD THE KEY TO HAPPINESS

In a world where happiness shines so bright,
Unhappy souls may try to dim its light.
But fear not, dear friend, for you hold the key,
To protect your joy and set your spirit free.

Walk away from those who sow despair,
Doomsayers and dream crushers, beware.
For their words may sting and bring you down,
But you have the power to turn it around.

Surround yourself with positivity and light,
Shield your mind from negativity's blight.
Nurture your body with love and care,
Embrace the moments that make life fair.

Protect your spirit, let it soar and fly,
In the face of darkness, let your joy defy.
Find solace in nature, in laughter, and song,
In the simple pleasures that keep you strong.

For happiness is a precious treasure to hold,
A flame that burns within, never to be sold.
So guard it fiercely, like a precious gem,
And let the unhappy souls fade into the hem.

Remember, dear friend, your happiness is yours,
To protect, to cherish, to explore.
Walk away from those who bring you down,
And let your spirit rise, wearing joy like a crown.

LOVING YOUR LIFE

In a world so vast and full of delight,
I find solace in loving my life so bright.
From the gentle breeze that caresses my face,
To the laughter of loved ones, filling every space.

I cherish the moments, both big and small,
For they are the building blocks of my life's grand hall.
A sunrise that paints the sky with hues so divine,
Reminds me to savor each moment, for it's truly one of a
kind.

The chirping of birds, a symphony in the air,
Teaches me to appreciate the beauty everywhere.
A playful kitten's antics, so full of joy,
Remember to embrace life's moments, never to be coy.

Through intention and manifestation, I create,
A life filled with love, joy, and abundant fate.
With gratitude in my heart, I attract what I desire,
Manifesting dreams that set my soul on fire.

The embrace of a loved one, so warm and true,
A reminder of the love that surrounds me, through and
through.
A heartfelt conversation, connecting souls so deep,
Fosters bonds that in my heart, I'll always keep.

In loving my life, I find peace and content,
Embracing each experience, wherever it's meant.
For life is a gift, a precious treasure to hold,
And in loving it fully, my spirit unfolds.

So let us celebrate the beauty that we find,
In every living creature, in every person kind.
For in loving our lives, we radiate a light so bright,
And create a world where love and joy ignite.

342

DIVERSITY IS BEAUTIFUL

In a world so diverse, where colors unfold,
It's vital to celebrate each unique soul.
For in the tapestry of life, woven with care,
The beauty of individuality is beyond compare.

From the graceful flight of a majestic bird,
To the intricate patterns on a butterfly's wings, absurd.
Each living creature, from land to sea,
Holds a beauty that sets them free.

The strength of a lion, fierce and bold,
Roaming the savannah, a story untold.
The delicate grace of a swan in a lake,
Gliding with elegance, its path will make.

A blooming flower, vibrant and rare,
Each petal is a masterpiece beyond compare.
The gentle whisper of wind through the trees,
A symphony of nature, dancing with ease.

In every person, a story unfolds,
A journey of triumphs and challenges untold.
The scars and the flaws that make them unique,
Are the very things that make hearts speak.

The laughter of a child, pure and true,
A reminder of innocence, anew.
The wisdom of an elder, weathered by time,
Their stories and experiences, a treasure sublime.

In celebrating uniqueness, we foster connection,
Embracing diversity, with love and affection.

For when we see beauty in every living being,
We create a world where harmony is freeing.

So let us celebrate, with open hearts and minds,
The beauty differences, that intertwines.
For it is in the celebration of uniqueness we find,
A world where love and acceptance are truly kind.

CREATE A FUTURE
THAT SETS YOU FREE

In the depths of your mind, a story unfolds,
A tale of mistakes and failures untold.
But listen closely, for I have found,
A truth that will turn your world around.

Stop telling yourself that old story, my friend,
The one that keeps your spirit penned.
For in those words, you cast your fate,
Creating barriers that suffocate.

Release the chains of past regret,
And set your soul on a new path, I bet.
The power lies within your hands,
To rewrite the script and take a stand.

Let go of what went wrong before,
Embrace the lessons and close that door.
For dwelling on the past will only bind,
Your dreams and aspirations left behind.

Instead, envision a future so bright,
Filled with possibilities, shining with light.
Tell yourself a story of resilience and grace,
A narrative that propels you to embrace.

Embrace the strength that lies within,
And let your true potential begin.
For you are the author of your own tale,
With the power to rewrite, to prevail.

Cast aside the doubts that hold you back,
And embark on a journey, leaving no track.
Create a story that's filled with delight,
Where your dreams take flight, reaching great height.

So, my dear friend, hear this decree,
Stop telling yourself that old story, you see.
For in the present, you hold the key,
To create a future that sets you free.

CELEBRATE YOUR OWN LIFE

In the shadows of yesterday's pain,
Lies a chance to rewrite, to reclaim.
For the story you tell is yours to mold,
A canvas of possibilities waiting to unfold.

Leave behind the regrets that cling tight,
And embrace the dawn of a brand-new light.
For in rewriting your own tale,
You have the power to prevail.

Imagine a protagonist filled with might,
Who conquers fears and takes flight.
No longer bound by past mistakes,
They rise above, for their spirit awakes.

Like a phoenix rising from the ash,
You too can break free from the past's harsh lash.
Let go of the chapters that weigh you down,
And create a future where joy is found.

For every failure, a lesson learned,
A steppingstone on which wisdom is earned.
The pain and heartache, they shape your soul,
But they don't define you, they don't control.

Rewrite your story with courage and zest,
Embrace the challenges, put them to the test.
Let go of the doubts that hold you back,
And forge a path on a different track.

Just like a caterpillar becomes a butterfly,
You too can transform, reach for the sky.

Leave behind the cocoon of yesterday,
And spread your wings, in vibrant display.

So, rewrite your story, let it unfold,
With chapters of resilience and stories untold.
For you hold the pen, the power to create,
A tale of strength, love, and endless debate.

Let's rewrite your own story,
Could be leaving behind a toxic relationship's glory.
Or choosing a career that sets your soul on fire,
Instead of settling for what others desire.

Perhaps it's forgiving yourself for past mistakes,
And embracing self-love, for your own sake.
Or letting go of the fear of the unknown,
And stepping into a world where dreams are sown.

So, my friend, seize this chance to rewrite,
Your story, your journey, in vibrant light.
Leave behind the regrets, the pain, and the strife,
And create a narrative that celebrates your life.

TO MY LOVING PARENTS
AND SIBLINGS

In a world filled with love and grace,
I find solace in your warm embrace.
For you, my dear parents, I pen this rhyme,
To express my gratitude, in prose and chime.

My loving father Fausto a man of faith so true,
With a heart of gratitude, shining through.
You taught me to believe in something higher,
To find strength in times of trial and fire.

And my loving mother, Jenny, a visionary soul,
With a vision that made our family whole.
Your unwavering spirit, a guiding light,
Leading us through both the day and night.

To Maria, the eldest girl so wise,
A sister, a wife, and a friend, a precious prize.
You showed me strength and resilience,
Guiding us through life's bewildering maze

And Francisco, the oldest boy so kind,
A protector and guide, always there to bind.
Your love and support, solid ground,
In your embrace, true comfort found.

To Zulema, Sergio and Ruben siblings dear,
In your love, I find solace and cheer.
With gratitude in my heart, I stand,
Forever blessed, holding your hands.

So today, with heartfelt words I say,
Thank you, dear parents, every day.
For love, the lessons, and the years,
For wiping away every tear.

EMBRACING SELF-CARE

In a world that spins with relentless pace,
Where chaos abounds, and stress we chase,
There lies a path, serene and bright,
A journey inward, to find our light.

Enter self-care, a gentle embrace,
Practice that brings us solace and grace.
Among its treasures, yoga stands tall,
A union of body, mind, and soul enthralled.

With each asana, a dance of strength,
We find balance, a harmonious length.
From downward dog to warrior's pose,
We stretch and breathe, our worries dispose.

In the stillness of a calming breath,
We release tension, bidding it death.
As we flow through a sun salutation,
Our bodies awakened, a vibrant sensation.

Yoga teaches patience, a priceless gift,
As we hold poses, our minds begin to lift.
We learn to let go, to surrender control,
Embracing the present, nourishing the soul.

In tree pose, we find stability and roots,
Connecting to Earth, shedding life's disputes.
Like a tree swaying in the gentle breeze,
We find strength within, our worries appease.

And in the depths of peaceful meditation,
We discover clarity, a divine revelation.

The mind becomes still, the chatter subsides,
As we delve within, where peace resides.

Yoga is a practice, not just on the mat,
It's a way of life, where self-love is at.
It reminds us to nourish our bodies and minds,
To prioritize ourselves, for the benefits we find.

Through self-care and yoga, we cultivate bliss,
A sense of well-being, a state of pure bliss.
We find resilience, a calmness that endures,
In the midst of life's storms, our spirit reassures.

So let us embrace self-care, with open hearts,
And let yoga guide us, as it imparts,
The benefits of practice are so profound,
A journey inward, where true peace is found.

LOVE, HEALTH & HAPPINESS

In a world that craves love, health, and bliss,
Commitment to happiness, a radical twist.
For in this quest, a profound truth we find,
That our light of joy can illuminate mankind.

To commit to love, a transformative act,
A choice to embrace, to never retract.
In tender moments and passionate embrace,
We build connections, weaving love's grace.

Like a ripple in water, love expands,
Touching hearts, bridging distant lands.
In acts of kindness, compassion prevails,
Love's power, a force that never fails.

Committing to health, a sacred vow,
Nurturing our bodies, here and now.
Through nourishing meals and daily care,
We honor the vessel we've been given to bear.

In the sweat of exercise, we find release,
A vibrant energy, a newfound peace.
With every step and breath, we take,
Our bodies strengthen; vitality awake.

To commit to happiness, a radical choice,
A beacon of light, a resounding voice.
For when we embrace our joy within,
Our radiance shines, dispelling shadows so thin.

In laughter's embrace, we find pure delight,
A symphony of mirth, a soul's true flight.

Through simple pleasures, big and small,
Happiness blossoms, embracing us all.

And as we commit to love, health, and bliss,
Our happiness becomes a guiding abyss.
It doesn't threaten, nor does it sway,
Instead, it lights the way, come what may.

For in the darkness, a single spark,
Can ignite a flame, dispel the dark.
And as we commit to happiness, we see,
It's contagious, spreading love's decree.

So let us embrace this radical notion,
And commit to love, health, and devotion.
For in doing so, we create a world so bright,
Where happiness shines, a beacon of light.

REACHING FOR THE STARS

In pursuit of dreams, I set my sights high,
Not seeking balance but reaching for the sky.
With fiery passion and relentless drive,
I embarked on a journey, ready to thrive.

"I didn't set out to achieve balance," I exclaimed,
But to make my dreams a reality, untamed.
For balance, though serene, can sometimes bind,
Restricting the wild spirit that resides in my mind.

With audacity and courage, I forged my own path,
Unafraid to veer from the trodden aftermath.
I embraced the chaos, the ups and downs,
Knowing that through it all, growth abounds.

Unfettered by the notion of perfect equilibrium,
I dared to venture into the unknown, my freedom.
For it is in the pursuit of big dreams we find,
The exhilaration of life, leaving no dreams behind.

Through sleepless nights and tireless days,
I worked relentlessly, pushing the boundaries away.
I faced challenges head-on, with unwavering will,
Determined to conquer and rise higher still.

And as I pursued those dreams, relentless and bold,
I discovered a truth worth more than gold.
That balance, though elusive, can be found,
In the moments of triumph, profound.

For the joy of achievement, a symphony of delight,
Brings harmony and balance, shining so bright.

I didn't set out to achieve balance, it's true,
But in making dreams come alive, balance ensues.

So let us not be confined by the notion of balance,
But embrace the journey, take a chance.
For in the pursuit of dreams, unbridled and vast,
We find the balance we seek, that will forever last.

WOMEN'S SEXUALITY

In the realm of sexuality, age knows no bounds,
A birthright cherished, where pleasure resounds.
For there is no ceiling to the depths we can explore,
Examples abound, showcasing the spirit's allure.

In the twilight years, love's flame still burns bright,
Passion ignites, defying age's might.
An elderly couple, hands clasped in embrace,
Discovering new realms, a love that won't erase.

In the blossoming youth, desires awaken,
Exploring their bodies, love's foundation shaken.
Two souls intertwined, discovering their bliss,
Unleashing their spirits, a tender, passionate kiss.

Across the spectrum of gender and identity,
Sexuality thrives, in all its diversity.
From a woman's touch to a man's caress,
From same-sex love to a non-binary address.

In the realm of sexuality, power dynamics at play,
Exploring boundaries, consent leading the way.
From dominant to submissive, pleasure unfolds,
A tapestry of desires, as the story unfolds.

In the realm of polyamory, love knows no bounds,
Multiple hearts entwined, where trust abounds.
Exploring connections, building love's bridge,
Embracing the spirit of freedom, without a smidge.

From the solo explorers, self-pleasure divine,
Masturbation's embrace, a personal shrine.

The power of self-love, an intimate affair,
Nurturing the spirit, in moments of care.
Let us celebrate the limitless expanse,
Of sexuality's journey, a beautiful dance.
There is no ceiling, no boundaries to constrain,
For pleasure and love, forever shall reign.

AN AGELESS GODDESS

In the realm where desires ignite,
Where Venus dances, pure and bright,
Unveiling powers deeply woven,
A tapestry of passion, freely woven.

Woman, an enigma, a force untamed,
Her sexuality, a flame unashamed,
A symphony of curves, a celestial art,
Unleashing love's fire, straight from the heart.

Venus, the goddess, her essence divine,
Unplugged, she rises, her spirit aligns,
With every touch, an awakening bloom,
A dance of pleasure, dispelling all gloom.

In her embrace, the world comes alive,
She nurtures passions, helps them thrive,
Her sensuality, a gateway to explore,
A sacred realm, forevermore.

In her whispers, secrets intertwine,
Unleashing desires, both yours and mine,
She embraces pleasure without restraint,
A celebration of love, without complaint.

Her spirit, wild and beautifully free,
Unveiling truths that only she can see,
Her sexuality, a force that undulates,
A power that resonates, never abates.

So let us honor the goddess within,
Embrace her fire, let the love begin,

For women's sexuality, a gift so pure,
A testament to love's allure.

SEX AND SPIRIT

In the realm of passion's fire,
Lies the power of women's desire.
A force that burns with fierce intensity,
Unleashing a captivating femininity.

With every sway of her hips,
She ignites a symphony of whispers and tips.
Her confidence, a magnet that draws,
Intriguing minds and breaking societal laws.

She is the embodiment of sensuality,
A muse of divine femininity.
From Cleopatra's seductive gaze,
To Frida Kahlo's unapologetic ways.

Like Marilyn Monroe's sultry allure,
Or Maya Angelou's words that endure,
Women's sexuality transcends boundaries,
Shattering limitations and societal confinities.

From the boldness of Josephine Baker's dance,
To the defiance in Malala Yousafzai's stance,
Women have harnessed the power within,
To challenge norms and let their desires begin.

In the bedroom, she claims her throne,
Her pleasure, a language all her own.
She knows her body, its curves and delight,
Embracing pleasure without guilt or spite.

Through intimacy, she finds her voice,
In the depths of passion, she makes her choice.

She celebrates her desires, unafraid,
Creating a world where her pleasure is laid.

For women's sexuality is a sacred gift,
A source of strength that causes spirits to lift.
It holds the power to heal and create,
To connect souls and transcend fate.

Let us honor and celebrate,
The power of women's sexuality, innate.
For in its embrace, we find liberation and grace,
A testament to the beauty of the feminine embrace.

ICONIC WOMEN

In the tapestry of time, there exist,
Iconic women who have dared to resist.
Challenging societal norms with fervor,
Embracing their sexuality, forever.

Frida Kahlo, a painter bold and true,
Her art a reflection of her desires anew.
With vibrant strokes, she bared her soul,
Defying conventions, taking control.

Josephine Baker, a dancer unparalleled,
Her sensuality, a story to be upheld.
Onstage, she moved with grace and flair,
Breaking boundaries, leaving the world in a stare.

Marilyn Monroe, an epitome of allure,
Her sexuality a symbol pure.
She embraced her curves, her beauty divine,
A beacon of sensuality, forever enshrined.

Audre Lorde, a poetess fierce and strong,
Her words spoke of liberation's song.
With verses that challenged societal norms,
She empowered women in all forms.

Gloria Steinem, an advocate for change,
Her voice resonated, refusing to estrange.
She fought for equality, breaking through,
Inspiring generations, both old and new.

Madonna, a pop queen without compare,
Her sexuality, a declaration to bear.

Unapologetically, she pushed the boundaries,
Empowering women through her melodies.

These iconic women, they paved the way,
For others to embrace their truth and sway.
They shattered expectations, defied the mold,
Leaving a legacy that will never grow old.

So let us honor these women of might,
Who challenged norms and took flight.
Their embrace of sexuality, a beacon of light,
Guiding us towards a future, shining bright.

OUR EROTIC ANATOMY

In a world where shame is cast aside,
Let's celebrate self-pleasure, with nothing to hide.
Embracing power within our own hand,
Unleashing desires, a journey so grand.

For women's sexuality is a sacred flame,
A force that should never be tamed.
In the realm of pleasure, a rightful domain,
Where joy and fulfillment forever remain.

With each touch, each caress, a symphony unfolds,
As pleasure cascades, our spirits behold.
The power of self-pleasure, a gift so divine,
Unlocking desires, letting our souls shine.

In the sanctuary of self, we find solace and peace,
A moment to connect, to let inhibitions release.
For female sexuality holds the key,
To our own happiness, our souls set free.

Unlimited pleasure, a birthright we claim,
A celebration of desires, unburdened by shame.
In the sacred realm of self-pleasure's embrace,
We honor ourselves and find our own grace.

So let us revel in the pleasures we seek,
Without judgment or stigma, let our spirits speak.
For shame-free self-pleasure is a path to explore,
A journey of self-love that forever restores.

In the realm of ultimate self-pleasure's embrace,
We find liberation, in each loving trace.

For female sexuality is a force to be revered,
A source of joy that should never be feared.

Claim your pleasure, with confidence and might,
Embrace the power within, let your desires take flight.
For unlimited pleasure is your birthright, dear friend,
In the realm of self-pleasure, may your happiness never end.

A PLEASURABLE CREATOR

In the sacred temple of our being,
Lies a portal, a source of infinite seeing.
Our vagina, a vessel of creation and pleasure,
A sacred space where magic and energy treasure.

Oh, how it holds the power to ignite,
The flames of passion, burning so bright.
A pleasurable creator, a gateway divine,
Unleashing desires, a union so fine.

Embracing the essence of sex magic's allure,
We harness creative energy, vibrant and pure.
Through touch, through intimacy, we connect,
A dance of pleasure, a soulful duet.

To give and receive, delicate art,
A symphony of sensations, a rhythm to start.
Exploring the depths of pleasure's embrace,
We find ecstasy, in each loving trace.

For the goddess of sexual pleasure resides within,
A divine force, unapologetic, ready to begin.
With laughter and joy, we embark on this quest,
To honor our desires, to be fully blessed.

So let us revel in the pleasures we share,
With open hearts, without a care.
In the realm of sexual pleasure, we thrive,
As goddesses of pleasure, we come alive.

With every breath, every moan, we soar,
In the realm of passion, forevermore.

For our sacred portal, our vagina, holds the key,
To unlock our power, our true ecstasy.

So let us celebrate, with reverence and delight,
The beauty of pleasure, both day and night.
For in the realm of sex magic, we find bliss,
A journey of pleasure, sealed with a kiss.

Embrace your inner goddess, let her shine,
In the realm of pleasure, let her define.
For our sacred portal is a gateway divine,
A source of pleasure, where magic intertwine.

A VESSEL OF GRACE

In the depths of our being, where strength resides,
Lies a power untamed, where life's force abides.
Our pelvis bowl, a vessel of grace,
Holding the secrets of our sacred space.

Within this sacred vessel, stories unfold,
Of strength and resilience, of tales untold.
The power of our pelvis, a force so profound,
An anchor of stability, where balance is found.

Like the roots of a tree, firmly planted below,
Our pelvis supports us, helping us grow.
It cradles our organs, our center of life,
A sacred container, free from strife.

In childbirth, it opens, wide and strong,
Bringing forth life, a miracle so long.
The pelvis, a gateway, where creation begins,
A testament to the strength of our kin.

In dance, it sways, a rhythm divine,
Expressing emotions, a language so fine.
It moves with grace, in sync with the beat,
A powerful force, a rhythm complete.

In lovemaking, it pulses, a dance so intimate,
Connecting bodies, souls intertwined in the moment.
The pelvis, a vessel, where pleasure resides,
Unleashing desires, where passion collides.

In yoga and movement, it finds its flow,
Allowing energy to circulate and grow.

The pelvis, a channel, where life force flows,
A source of vitality, where transformation shows.
So let us honor the power of our pelvis bowl,
With gratitude and reverence, body and soul.
For within its depths, lies strength untold,
A sacred space, where power unfolds.

Embrace the power of your pelvis, dear friend,
For it holds the magic, from beginning to end.
In its grace and strength, let your spirit rise,
And unleash the power that within you lies.

YOU ARE A MASTERPIECE!

In the mirror's gaze, behold the divine,
A goddess stands before you, radiant and fine.
No need for comparison or seeking perfection,
For within you lies beauty in every direction.

Embrace the curves that grace your form,
Each line and contour, a masterpiece born.
Your body, a canvas, where artistry resides,
A reflection of the universe's infinite tides.

Your eyes, like sparkling gems, hold a universe within,
Reflecting strength and wisdom, where stories begin.
The windows to your soul, shining bright and clear,
Revealing the depths of your essence, pure and sincere.

Your smile, a beacon of joy and delight,
Illuminating the world with its radiant light.
It speaks of laughter, of love, and of grace,
A testament to the beauty that adorns your face.

Your voice, a melody, like a soothing song,
A symphony of power, gentle yet strong.
With every word you speak, you inspire and empower,
A goddess's essence, a divine flower.

Your spirit, a flame that burns with passion and fire,
Guiding you through life's journey, higher and higher.
In your authenticity, you find strength and power,
A goddess' presence, in every waking hour.

Embrace the beauty that lies within your soul,
For you are a goddess, unique and whole.

No need for comparison or changing who you are,
For your essence shines brightly, like a radiant star.

So celebrate yourself, goddess divine,
Embrace your uniqueness, let your light shine.
For you are a masterpiece, a work of art,
A goddess, just as you are, from the very start.

EMBRACE THE PLEASURE

In the realm of touch, where pleasure resides,
Let instincts guide us, where passion collides.
Embrace the sensations, both tender and bold,
A symphony of pleasure, ageless and untold.

In the warmth of a companion's loving embrace,
We find solace and comfort, a sacred space.
Together we dance, our bodies entwined,
As pleasure ignites, leaving worries behind.

Caresses gentle, like whispers on the skin,
Stirring desires, awakening from within.
Fingers tracing pathways of delightful delight,
Exploring new realms in the depths of the night.

In the realm of touch, let pleasure be our guide,
With every stroke and kiss, let passion collide.
Savor the moments, indulge in the bliss,
For pleasure knows no boundaries, no age to dismiss.

Let go of inhibitions, release all control,
As pleasure takes over, body and soul.
In the realm of touch, we find liberation,
A celebration of pleasure, without hesitation.

For pleasure knows no limits, no societal norms,
It's a language we speak, in intimate forms.
Listen to your instincts, they know what's true,
In the realm of touch, let pleasure ensue.

So, embrace the pleasure, both tender and wild,
Let go of judgments, let passion be styled.

MARIA L. ELLIS

In the dance of touch, find ecstasy's treasure,
For pleasure is timeless, a source of pure pleasure.

SURRENDER TO PLEASURE

In the realm of pleasure, surrender we must,
To the intoxicating waves, the desires that thrust.
Let go of inhibitions, embrace the unknown,
And let pleasure guide us, in a world of its own.

Like the warmth of the sun on a summer's day,
Basking in pleasure, in its radiant display.
A gentle touch that ignites a fire within,
As fingertips dance on skin, a sensuous spin.

Like the taste of chocolate, rich and divine,
Melting on the tongue, a moment so fine.
Indulging in pleasure, savoring each bite,
As it takes us on a journey, a delicious delight.

Like the sound of music, a symphony of bliss,
As melodies caress, in a passionate kiss.
The rhythm of pleasure, enticing and sweet,
Guiding us in a dance, where ecstasy meets.

Like the scent of roses, enchanting the air,
A fragrance that whispers, "come, if you dare."
Inhaling the pleasure, intoxicating and pure,
A sensory journey, where fantasies allure.

Like the sight of stars, twinkling above,
In the darkness of night, a canvas of love.
Gazing at pleasure, in its ethereal glow,
As it paints desires, that only we know.

Surrender to pleasure, let it take the lead,
In its tender embrace, fulfill all our needs.

For pleasure is a gift, to be cherished and explored,
A symphony of sensations, where we are adored.

BRING SACRED INTO
YOUR SEXUALITY

In the realm of passion, let the sacred reside,
Unveiling desires, with nothing to hide.
Embrace the divine, in the dance of two souls,
In the sacred union, where love truly unfolds.

Let the whispers of reverence guide your touch,
As you explore each other, in moments so lush.
Awakening the senses, igniting the flame,
In the sacred space, where pleasure finds its name.

Breathe in the essence, of the sacred divine,
Let it infuse your being, as passion intertwines.
Embrace your power, let inhibitions fade,
For in the sacred union, you are beautifully made.

In every tender caress, feel the sacred energy flow,
Connecting on a level, only lovers can know.
Let go of the mundane, step into the sublime,
As you merge your spirits, beyond space and time.

In the sacred union, find liberation and grace,
Embrace your sexuality, in its fullest embrace.
Release the chains that hold you back,
And experience pleasure, in its rawest track.

For pleasure is sacred, a gift to be revered,
In the depths of passion, where ecstasy is steered.
Open your heart, let love be your guide,
And empower your sexuality, with nothing to hide.

Create a sanctuary, where pleasure can bloom,
In the sacred space, where desires consume.
Make room for pleasure, let it take its place,
For in the sacred union, you find solace and grace.

So, embrace the sacred, let it dance with desire,
In the realm of passion, let your spirits soar higher.
Empower your sexuality, let pleasure reign supreme,
And awaken the divine, in your most intimate dream.

LOVE YOURSELF!

In a world that seeks conformity, dare to be bold,
For within you lie a story, waiting to be told.
You are a masterpiece, a creation like no other,
An ageless goddess, with infinite power to discover.

Embrace the mirror, with eyes full of love,
See the beauty within, shining from above.
Let go of the doubts, the judgments, the strife,
For you are a beacon of light, in this journey called life.

With courage as your armor, and self-love as your guide,
Embrace your uniqueness, let your spirit glide.
Celebrate your flaws, they make you who you are,
A tapestry of experiences, both near and far.

You are a symphony, a melody so divine,
With every note, your essence begins to shine.
Unleash your passions, let them radiate,
For you hold the power to create your own fate.

In the depths of your soul, find the love you seek,
Embrace your worthiness, let your spirit speak.
For you are deserving, of love and all things kind,
A goddess, ageless and beautifully aligned.

Cherish the temple, that is your earthly vessel,
Nurture it with love, let it bloom and nestle.
For within your being, lies a universe untold
A sacred space, where your worth will unfold.

Embrace your uniqueness, with every breath you take,
For you are a goddess, a love that will not break.

Have the courage to love yourself, fiercely and true,
And watch as the world mirrors that love back to you.

LIVE FROM A
HEART-CENTERED PLACE

In the realm of connection, where souls intertwine,
Lies the power of co-creation, a partnership divine.
With hearts as our compass, guiding the way,
We embark on a journey, where love holds sway.

In a co-creative partnership, we join hands and minds,
Combining our strengths, our passions entwined.
Together we weave a tapestry, vibrant and bright,
As we dance through life, guided by love's light.

From a heart-centered place, we create and inspire,
Fueled by the flame of love, burning higher and higher.
Bound by trust and respect, our energies entwine,
As we manifest dreams, one heartbeat at a time.

With open hearts, we listen and understand,
Supporting each other, hand in hand.
In this sacred union, we challenge and grow,
Nurturing the seeds of love we sow.

Through the power of cocreation, we find harmony,
Balancing our individuality with unity.
We celebrate each other's uniqueness and grace,
Honoring the beauty of our shared space.

In this partnership, the world becomes our canvas,
A playground for love, where dreams do not vanish.
With courage and vulnerability, we step into the unknown,
Creating a legacy of love, uniquely our own.

So let us embrace the power of co-creative bliss,
Living from a heart center, where love truly exists.
Together we can transform, inspire, and mend,
For in partnership, our souls find a love that will transcend.

LIFE LIVED FULLY

In the realm of dreams, where possibilities reside,
Lies a philosophy that fills my heart with pride.
To dream my life as if I'll live to be 112,
To embrace each day as if it's brand new.

With hope as my guide, I'll envision a life,
Filled with health and happiness, free from strife.
I'll paint a canvas of vitality in my mind,
Creating a future where joy and wellness intertwine.

From the moment I wake, with gratitude I'll rise,
Embracing the day with wonder in my eyes.
For this day, the one I wake up in,
Is a precious gift, a chance to begin.

I'll cherish each breath, each beat of my heart,
Living fully present, embracing every part.
With a zest for life, I'll seize every opportunity,
Embracing adventure, with curiosity as my key.

I'll nourish my body, mind, and soul,
Making choices that make me whole.
With mindful care, I'll tend to my well-being,
Creating a foundation for a life worth seeing.

But it's not just about me, this philosophy I hold,
For in the journey of life, we are never alone.
I'll inspire others with my vibrant spirit,
Encouraging them to dream and believe it.

Together we'll create a world of boundless dreams,
Where age is just a number, and possibility gleams.

With joy as our compass, we'll navigate each day,
Living fully, making every moment count in every way.

Let's dream our lives, as if we'll live to be 112,
Embracing each day, letting our spirits ascend.
For in the power of now, the present we find,
A life lived fully, with love intertwined.

YOU HAVE THE POWER TO CHANGE

In the realm of possibility, you hold the key,
To change the course of your destiny.
With small adjustments or grand shifts,
You have the power to uplift.

Clarity is the compass that guides your way,
Defining your goals, day by day.
With a clear vision, you set your intention,
And embark on a journey of transformation.

But it's not just excitement that starts the race,
It's the action you take at a steady pace.
Showing up, putting in the work,
To create the life, you truly deserve.

Breaking bad habits, a noble pursuit,
Replacing them with actions that bear fruit.
Abundance awaits, if you believe,
And take the steps to achieve.

A change in career, a bold endeavor,
To find fulfillment that lasts forever.
With focus and determination, you'll find,
A path that aligns with your heart and mind.

So dream big and aim high,
With every effort, you'll reach the sky.
Remember, the power to change resides within,
Embrace it fully and let your journey begin.

CREATE THE LIFE
YOU TRULY DESERVE

To craft the life you truly deserve,
There are actions you must bravely serve.
It starts with a vision, clear and bright,
Guiding your steps, both day and night.

First, believe in yourself, without a doubt,
For self-belief is what it's all about.
Embrace your worth, your unique voice,
And let your dreams be your empowered choice.

Next, set your goals, both big and small,
With clarity, write them down, stand tall.
Break them into steps, achievable and clear,
And watch as your path begins to appear.

Take action boldly, don't hesitate,
For progress thrives when you participate.
Each day, commit to tasks that align,
With the life you envision, so divine.

Embrace resilience, when challenges arise,
For setbacks are an opportunity in disguise.
Learn from them, adapt, and persevere,
And watch your strength and courage appear.

Surround yourself with those who inspire,
Whose support and love set your soul on fire.
Build a tribe of kindred spirits, true,
Who uplifts and encourage the best in you.
Nurture your mind, body, and soul,

With self-care rituals that make you whole.
Prioritize rest, and listen within,
For self-care is where true growth begins.

Embrace gratitude, in every single day,
Find joy in the simple things that come your way.
Celebrate your wins, big and small,
And let gratitude be your guiding call.

And finally, remember to give back,
Spread kindness and love along your track.
For as you uplift others, you'll find,
Your own light shines brighter, refined.

Take these actions, with purpose and heart,
And watch as your life transforms into art.
Create the life you truly deserve,
With every step, let your dreams be preserved.

OPPORTUNITIES FOR GROWTH AND STRENGTH

In the face of setbacks and challenges, we find,
Opportunities for growth, strength intertwined.
For life's journey is not always smooth and clear,
But through adversity, we can persevere.

When hurdles appear, blocking our way,
We must not let discouragement hold sway.
Instead, let us embrace these trials we face,
For within them, lies wisdom and grace.

Setbacks are not signs of defeat or despair,
But chances to learn, to rise and repair.
They test our resolve, our resilience and might,
And show us the depths of our inner light.

Through challenges, our strength is honed,
Like a diamond, shaped and beautifully toned.
We discover depths we never knew we possessed,
And find the courage to face any test.

Each obstacle we encounter on our path,
Is an opportunity to grow and surpass.
To push beyond limits, to strive and ascend,
And emerge stronger, with a spirit on the mend.

In the face of adversity, we learn to adapt,
To find new perspectives, to bridge the gap.
We uncover hidden strengths, waiting to be found,
And rise above, standing firmly on solid ground.

So let us not fear setbacks and strife,
But embrace them as catalysts for a new life.
For it is through challenges, we truly see,
The immense power that lies within you and me.

So when life throws hurdles, stand tall and strong,
Know that setbacks are where resilience belongs.
Embrace the lessons, the growth they bestow,
And watch as your strength and resilience grow.

For setbacks and challenges, though they may be tough,
Are the steppingstones that make us enough.
So with an open heart and unwavering belief,
Embrace the opportunities for growth and relief.

CREATING A LIFE, YOU LOVE

In the realm of possibility, where dreams come alive,
There lies a secret to a life we truly thrive.
It's about raising your vibration, igniting your soul,
To create a life you love, to reach your ultimate goal.

With every breath you take, let positivity flow,
Release the negativity, let it all go.
For in the depths of your being, there's a power untold,
To manifest your desires, to create a life bold.

Raise your vibration, let your energy soar,
Unleash your passion, let your spirit explore.
Align with the universe, dance with the stars,
Embrace the magic, break through the bars.

Let go of limiting beliefs that hold you back,
Embrace the abundance that you now attract.
Shift your mindset, let gratitude lead the way,
And watch as your life transforms, day by day.

Surround yourself with love, with joyful hearts,
Connect with kindred spirits, where friendship imparts.
Raise your vibration through acts of kindness and care,
And watch as love and joy become your daily affair.

Nurture your body, mind, and spirit as one,
Feed your soul with experiences that make you feel alive.
Embrace the present moment, let go of the past,
And watch as your life becomes a beautiful contrast.

Create a vision, set intentions with clarity,
Believe in your dreams, embrace your authenticity.

Raise your vibration, let your inner light shine,
And watch as the universe aligns, in perfect rhyme.

For a life you love living, it starts from within,
Raise your vibration, let your journey begin.
Embrace the power that resides deep in your core,
And watch as your dreams manifest, forevermore.

Raise your vibration and let your spirit soar,
Embrace the love, the joy, the abundance galore.
Create a life you love, where dreams come true,
For raising your vibration is the key to you.

IGNITING YOUR SOUL

In the realm of creativity, we find our sacred space,
Where colors dance and words embrace,
A sanctuary where souls ignite,
With joy and fulfillment shining bright.

With brush in hand, we paint our dreams,
On canvas, a world of endless themes,
Abstract strokes and vibrant hues,
Expressing emotions, revealing truths.

Through the lens, a story unfolds,
Capturing moments, untold stories, untold,
Photographs freeze time's fleeting grace,
A glimpse of beauty, in every trace.

In the written word, we find solace,
Poetic verses, a language to embrace,
With pen and paper, we weave our tale,
Imagination soars, as words set sail.

The stage is set, the curtain rises,
Actors embody characters, wearing disguises,
Dramatic tales, emotions unfurled,
Theater's magic, touching the world.

In song and melody, our hearts align,
Music's rhythm, a language divine,
Voices soar, instruments play,
Elevating spirits, in harmony's sway.

Pottery wheels spin, clay takes shape,
Molding vessels, hopes and escapes,

From earth's embrace, creations arise,
Crafted with love, they mesmerize.

With needles and thread, we sew and mend,
Stitching fabrics, fashioning trends,
Fashion's artistry, a style all our own,
Clothing our bodies, confidence sown.

In gardens, we plant, with tender care,
Nurturing life, fresh scents in the air,
Blooms unfurl, petals open wide,
Nature's masterpiece, a joyous stride.

Engaging in creative activities, a gift bestowed,
Enriching our lives, a vibrant ode,
For in these moments, our souls awake,
In joy and fulfillment, we find our place.

CONSCIOUS MANIFESTATION

In realms of thought, where mysteries unfold,
Consciousness manifests, a story yet untold.
A tapestry of thoughts, woven with grace,
A symphony of ideas, filling up the space.

In dreams, it dances, creating vivid scenes,
A kaleidoscope of colors, painting vibrant dreams.
The mind's theater, where fantasies reside,
Consciousness takes flight, on wings so wide.

In art, it blooms, expressing boundless emotion,
A canvas alive, with strokes of devotion.
From brush to paper, from clay to stone,
Consciousness manifests, in forms unknown.

In love, it blossoms, a flame that ignites,
Connecting souls, with pure delight.
A gentle touch, a heartfelt smile,
Consciousness intertwines, beyond the mile.

In science, it ventures, seeking to explore,
Unraveling the universe, from shore to shore.
From atoms to galaxies, the mysteries unfold,
Consciousness awakens, truths yet untold.

In nature, it thrives, in every living being,
From majestic mountains to rivers serene.
A symphony of life, in harmony it sings,
Consciousness manifests in all living things.

In meditation, it finds solace and peace,
A serene sanctuary, where worries cease.

A moment of stillness, a mindful retreat,
Consciousness expands, in moments so sweet.

In every moment, in every breath we take,
Consciousness manifests, in choices we make.
From the grandest of ideas, to the smallest of sparks,
Consciousness is the essence that lights up the dark.

Let's embrace this wondrous creation,
The beauty of consciousness, in every manifestation.
For it is through awareness, that we truly see,
The infinite possibilities, of what we can be.

YOU ARE, WHAT YOU SPEAK

In words we find the power to express,
The essence of who we are, nothing less.
For language is the vessel that carries our identity,
A tapestry woven with words, for all to see.

With each syllable spoken, a story unfolds,
The richness of culture, the tales of old.
Through language, we establish our roots,
Connecting to our heritage, like sturdy roots.

In accents and dialects, our origins reside,
A map of our journey, where we've thrived.
From the rolling "r" of a Spanish tongue,
To the lilting tones of an Irish song.

Through language, we affirm our place,
Our unique voice, our distinct embrace.
With every word, we assert our truth,
Revealing our essence, like a vibrant hue.

In the words we choose, we shape our thoughts,
Crafting meaning, expressing our lots.
From poetry to prose, from songs to verse,
Language empowers; it's a gift we rehearse.
Through idioms and sayings, we share wisdom,
Passed down through generations, a cherished system.
In phrases and metaphors, we find connection,
Binding us together, with shared affection.

Language preserves our heritage and lore,
Preserving our stories, forevermore.

In ancient tongues and mother tongues,
The echoes of our past, forever sung.

Through language, we build bridges of understanding,
Breaking down barriers, compassion expanding.
In translation and interpretation, we find unity,
Embracing diversity, celebrating each community.

Let's cherish the power of speech,
For language is the key, within our reach.
It shapes our identity, it tells our tale,
With every word spoken, our essence unveiled.

THE CHOICES WE MAKE

In the tapestry of life, our choices are woven,
Each one a thread, a story yet unspoken.
For every step we take, a path unfolds,
Shaping our journey, as destiny beholds.

In the morning's embrace, as dawn awakes,
We face a crossroads, decisions to make.
With each choice made, the door swings wide,
Revealing the possibilities that reside.

In the realm of action, our intentions align,
The choices we make, a reflection of our design.
With every word spoken, a ripple is cast,
Impacting the present, determining what will last.

In the realm of love, our hearts are the guide,
Choosing compassion, with arms stretched wide.
For in the kindness, we show, and the love we share,
Our daily choices echo, creating a world that's fair.

In the realm of dreams, our desires ignite,
Each decision made, propelling us to new heights.
For the choices we make, shape our destiny,
Unveiling the path to who we're meant to be.

In the realm of challenges, our strength is revealed,
Choosing resilience, as wounds are healed.
For the choices we make in moments of strife,
Shape our character and define our life.

In the realm of time, our moments unfold,
Choosing presence, embracing what we hold.

For the choices we make, in each passing day,
Compose the symphony of our life's grand display.

So let us be mindful, with each choice we embrace,
Aware of the impact, the path we trace.
For in the tapestry of life, our choices will reside,
Weaving a legacy, as we journey side by side.

OUR CHOICES OR OUR FATE?

In the realm of freedom, a question arises,
Are we truly masters, or mere pawns in disguises?
As we navigate life's vast tapestry,
Do we possess free will, or is it just fallacy?

Every day, choices like rivers flow,
A dance of options, from which we must sow.
But behind the scenes, a current unseen,
Predetermined forces, orchestrating the scene.

Within our bodies, the autonomic reigns,
Regulating functions, without our refrains.
The beating hearts, the breath we take,
Controlled by forces we cannot shake.

In the depths of our minds, neurons fire,
A symphony of thoughts intricately wired.
Yet governed by laws, of physics and chemistry,
Constraining the bounds of our supposed free decree.

Our genes, inherited, a script set in stone,
The blueprint of life, in which we're thrown.
Fixed at birth, unchangeable and true,
Impacting our choices, without a clue.

But amidst this web of predetermined fate,
A glimmer of freedom, we must not underrate.
For though we're bound by physical laws,
Within the realm of choice, a spark unfurls.

In the spaces between, where possibilities reside,
We find the power to shape, to decide.

To rise above the currents, predetermined and strong,
And carve our own path, where we belong.

So perhaps true freedom lies not in complete control,
But in the awareness of forces, taking their toll.
To navigate the currents, with conscious intent,
Embracing the choices, that we're truly meant.

Do we really have free will? The answer unclear,
A complex tapestry, woven with doubt and fear.
But in the realm of choice, let us strive and explore,
For in the pursuit of freedom, we can find so much more.

ACKNOWLEDGMENTS

This book is the culmination of many journeys — of self-discovery, creativity, and awakening. It was born from quiet moments of reflection, from the whispers of the soul, and from the profound realization that the essence of life lies in embracing all that we are — body, mind, and spirit.

I wish to express my deepest gratitude to all the women who have inspired me — those who have lived courageously, loved deeply, and expressed themselves without apology. You have reminded me that feminine power is not only strength, but grace; not only passion, but purpose.

To the readers who open these pages with open hearts — may these poems awaken in you a sense of beauty, joy, and sacred connection. May they remind you that pleasure, creativity, and love are divine expressions of who we are meant to be.

To my family and friends — thank you for your unwavering love, encouragement, and belief in my creative journey. You have been my grounding force and my wings of faith.

Finally, to the creative spirit that flows through all of us — the source of inspiration, truth, and transformation — I give thanks. May this collection serve as a gentle reminder that we are all creators, capable of shaping beauty, healing, and meaning through the art of being fully alive.

With love and gratitude,
Maria L. Ellis, BBA, MBA

ABOUT THE AUTHOR

Maria L. Ellis, BBA, MBA, is a seasoned investor, business leader, and educator with a deep passion for helping others build lasting wealth through real estate. With decades of experience spanning finance, entrepreneurship, and strategic investing, Maria has mentored countless individuals to take control of their financial futures and invest with clarity, confidence, and purpose.

She is the founder of a family real estate investment firm, where she and her team acquire, manage, and grow multi-family portfolios across thriving U.S. markets. Known for her practical wisdom, compassionate leadership, and values-based approach, Maria believes that real estate is not just about properties – it's about people, impact, and legacy.

Maria is also a published author of multiple books on entrepreneurship, wellness, longevity, and women's empowerment. Her writing reflects her life's mission: to educate, inspire, and empower others to live fully and invest wisely.

When she's not negotiating deals or guiding investors, Maria enjoys traveling with her family, mentoring the next generation, and living a purpose-driven life filled with service, joy, and growth.

Connect with Maria:
Email: mellis@fsacap.com
Mobile: 973-216-4181

ABOUT ELLIS PUBLISHING HOUSE

Ellis Publishing House presents the work and vision of bestselling author and educator Maria L. Ellis, BBA, MBA. Founded to bring clear, useful ideas to a wide readership, the imprint focuses on practical nonfiction with enduring value—finance and business, health and longevity, leadership, caregiving, real estate, and poetry—alongside the signature *Journey to Wellness, Freedom, and Legacy* series. Editions are available in English and Spanish across print, eBook, and audio.

Maria's career spans international banking, investment advising, and financial planning, experience that informs her grounded approach to money, leadership, and long-term well-being. A graduate of the Harvard Business School Owner/President Management program, she holds business degrees from the University of Massachusetts Amherst and has served in leadership and advisory roles across education and nonprofit boards. Her books and talks emphasize clarity, compassion, and action—helping readers make better decisions for themselves, their families, and their communities.

Ellis Publishing House exists to advance that mission: books that translate expertise into everyday tools, invite thoughtful reflection, and encourage readers to build not only success but also significance. The catalog includes guides to financial freedom, family business legacy planning, entrepreneurial health, longevity, real-estate investing, leadership, caregiving, and a poetry collection that celebrates life on earth.

In all of its publishing, Ellis Publishing House favors ideas with measurable impact, stories with heart, and designs made to last—work shaped by Maria L. Ellis's commitment to service, integrity, and accessible excellence.

OTHER BOOKS BY
ELLIS PUBLISHING HOUSE

Achieve Financial Freedom: The Road Map to Financial Success by Maria L. Ellis, BBA, MBA

Family Business Legacy Plan: The Ultimate Guide to Creating a Legacy for Your Family without Paying too Much in Taxes by Maria L. Ellis, BBA, MBA

Redefining Entrepreneurial Success: A Guide to a Healthy and Holistic Lifestyle by Maria L. Ellis, BBA, MBA

Longevity: Reinvent Yourself at Any Age by Maria L. Ellis, BBA, MBA

Life on Earth: Poetic Perspectives by Maria L. Ellis, BBA, MBA

Golf: A Course in Business: A Few Lessons Golf Can Teach Us About Management & Entrepreneurship by Maria L. Ellis, BBA, MBA

From Operator to Entrepreneur: Unlocking the Power of Visionary Leadership by Maria L. Ellis, BBA, MBA

Stolen Memories: A Journey Through Alzheimer's by Maria L. Ellis, BBA, MBA

Designing Your Longevity: A Personalized Blueprint for Thriving Longer with Energy, Purpose, and Vitality by Maria L. Ellis, BBA, MBA

Investing in Multifamily Real Estate: A Guide to Investing for Income, Impact, and Generational Wealth by Maria L. Ellis, BBA, MBA